Ghosts & Legends of Staffordshire & The Black Country

David Bell

COUNTRYSIDE BOOKS

NEWBURY, BERKSHIRE

First published 1994
© David Bell 1994

COUNTRYSIDE BOOKS
3 Catherine Road
Newbury, Berkshire

ISBN 1 85306 307 X

Produced through MRM Associates Ltd., Reading
Typeset by Designertype (Bath) Limited
Printed by J. W. Arrowsmith Ltd., Bristol

This book is dedicated to the Jones clan:

Rosemary who became my wife in 1961;
Roy and Rosemary Jones, Stephen and Christopher,
of Amington; Trevor Jones, of Hopwas and to the
memory of Richard Jones (1949–93), a fellow jazz
fan and a great brother-in-law

Ghosts & Legends of Staffordshire & The Black Country

•Longnor

•Grindon

ldon •Ilam
•
•Swinscoe
• Mayfield

Alton

• Uttoxeter

DERBYSHIRE

•Tutbury
Hanbury• \
Anslow
•Abbots Bromley •Shobnall
dmaston ⊙BURTON UPON TRENT

ugeley

rnwood •Elford
⊙LICHFIELD   LEICESTERSHIRE
Hopwas•
⊙TAMWORTH

Hartshill•

⊙BIRMINGHAM

Acknowledgements and Thanks

I would like to acknowledge help given by the following newspapers in compiling this book: *Staffordshire Evening Sentinel; Burton Daily Mail; Leek Post & Times; Cheadle Post & Times; Uttoxeter Post & Times; Cheadle & Tean Times; Newcastle Advertiser; Lichfield Mercury; Cannock Mercury; Chase Post; Tamworth Herald; Bidulph Chronicle; Wolverhampton Express & Star; Stone Newsletter; Birmingham Evening Mail; Wombourne View; Black Country Bugle; Tamworth Post; Burton Herald & Post*. I am also grateful to the helpful staff of various local branches of the Staffordshire libraries.

There are many individuals I wish to thank for help generously given. These include Ros Prince; John Godwin; Tim Cockin; Jenny Allsop; Jacky Ayre; Bernie Barton; Audrey Blount; Ray Bood; K. Booth; Ian W. Brown; Jacqueline Burton-Naylor; Trevor Buxton; Susan Critchlow; Wendy & Julie Crutchley; David Curwen; Nicholas Damsell; Gretta Earnest; Olga & Julia Eaton; Mrs Eaton; Vicky Evitt; Ray Fallows; Jim Foley; Margaret Foley; Frederick R. Gee; Denise Goddard; Ethel Gorton and Agnes Rae; Liz Greenwood; Harry Heath; Roy & Rosemary Jones; Christopher Jones; Stephen Jones; Lionel Lethbridge; Linda Littlewood; Mark Mellor; Stephen Morris; Kate Newton; Janis Priestly; M. A. Shore; Nigel Slater; Gladys Smith; Revd Geoff Startin; Roger Turner; Barry Vallens; Rosemary Vanstone; Gordon T. Varley; Ivan Vinnell; Celia Warren; Roy Whitfield and Alan Woodcock.

Introduction

STAFFORDSHIRE is a county of surprising variety and contrast. It includes rural farmland in the centre of the county as well as the conurbation of the Potteries, based on the six towns (not five as Arnold Bennett claimed) of Burslem, Fenton, Hanley, Longton, Stoke-on-Trent and Tunstall. It also has the wild moorlands to the north and west of Leek and the highest village in England. Dovedale, which everyone 'knows' is in Derbyshire, is actually half in Staffordshire, the river Dove forming the county boundary. In fact, one wit once wrote that the best parts of Derbyshire are in Staffordshire!

The south of the county still includes the ancient town of Tamworth, once the seat of Mercian kings, and the cathedral city of Lichfield. Prior to the local government re-organisation in 1974, it also included the Black Country towns of Bilston, Tipton, West Bromwich, Walsall and Wolverhampton. Thanks to the title of this book referring to Staffordshire *and* the Black Country, I have been able to restore these towns to the county from which they were annexed (or 'stolen' as many Staffordshire folk claim).

Staffordshire also includes the former royal hunting ground of Cannock Chase, the wooded Kinver Edge, and, as any serious beer-drinker knows, the town of Burton-upon-Trent. It contains quarries and cathedrals, coal mines and castles, power stations and stately homes. Its legends include Robin Hood and his lover Clorinda, the fairies of Cauldon Lowe, the awesome power of the reindeer horns used by dancers at Abbots Bromley, and ghosts that haunt graveyards, castle ruins, pubs and parks.

My own relationship with the county includes a very happy period in the 1970s when I was headmaster of a village school in north Staffordshire, and another connection which began in 1961 when I married a girl from the south of the county.

I have never seen or heard any of Staffordshire's ghosts, much though I'd like to. I was formerly rather dismissive of stories of supernatural hauntings, and believed that they all had a logical explanation. They were the result of the mind putting a ghostly interpretation on an unusual phenomenon, or, on other occasions, a projection of our own personal anxieties and fears. But the people who have told me their experiences – police officers, miners, nurses, farmers – have all been such sensible and down-to-earth folk that it is no longer possible for me to be so dogmatic. Many of the manifestations described here defy a rational gloss. I have been forced to become much more open-minded; you must make up your own mind when you have read the book.

David Bell
Autumn 1994

ABBOTS BROMLEY

'The Most Primitive Dance in Europe'

THE annual Horn Dance, which takes place in Abbots Bromley every September, is so old that its origins are lost in the mists of early history. It was described by Robert Plot in 1686, in his *Natural History of Staffordshire*, but the dance was ancient even then. The six pairs of reindeer antlers used in the dance are believed to be of native British origin, which means that they must date from before the 12th century when the native reindeer became extinct.

The antlers are now kept in the village church but the nature of the dance suggests that it predates Christianity, and was originally a magic rite associated with hunting and fertility. The Church was not always so accommodating; the 7th century Archbishop of Canterbury banned 'the going about as a stag, or putting on the head or horns of beasts, for this is devilish'. The dance was banned again during the Commonwealth of Oliver Cromwell.

The dance now takes place on 'Wakes Monday', which is the Monday following the first Sunday after 4th September. However, when Robert Plot described it in the 17th century, it was performed at Christmas, New Year and Twelfth Night. This leads scholars to believe that it was a winter solstice custom.

Twelve men perform the Horn Dance. Six of them are the horn bearers and carry the antlers which are mounted on wooden deer-heads, carved in the 16th century. The largest set of antlers has a span of 39 inches and weighs over 25 pounds; the others are slightly smaller, the smallest having a span of 29 inches and weighing $16^1/2$ pounds. Three of the heads are painted white and three black, although in Robert Plot's day they were white and red.

The other performers are a fool, a hobby-horse, a bow-man, a man in woman's clothes and known as Maid

9

Marian, a boy with a triangle and a musician with an accordion. Earlier musicians have played the violin, and before that the pipe and tabor.

Maid Marian wears a white veil and a dress reaching to the ground. She carries a stick and a wooden ladle in which she collects money. This man-dressed-as-woman character is known to predate the stories of Robin Hood's Maid Marian by many centuries. The fool wears a jester's motley, but the others all wear a costume of knee breeches, knitted green stockings and sleeveless jerkins of red, brown and gold. This costume appears authentically medieval, but was designed by a vicar's wife in 1880. Prior to that date, the dancers wore their own clothes, decorated with ribbons.

At 8.30 am on Wakes Monday, when the antlers have been fetched from the church, the twelve performers set out on a 20 mile tour of the parish, taking in grand houses, humble cottages and outlying farms. At each they stop and dance. It is widely believed that it would be bad luck to miss out any of the usual dancing places. The final dance is performed back in the village street.

The same set dance is performed each time. It begins with a silent single file of dancers who form a circle, which loops into a figure of eight. Then the music begins and the horn bearers face each other. They advance, appear to lock horns, and retreat. In an article written in 1933 Violet Alford described the Abbots Bromley Horn Dance as 'the most primitive dance in Europe'. The music is played by the accordionist, the beat emphasised by the boy playing his triangle, Maid Marian beating her stick and ladle together, the hobby-horse snapping his jaws, and the bow-man clapping his crossbow and arrow. Unfortunately, the tunes used are comparatively modern.

When the dancing is over, the horns are returned to the church and an evening of drinking and revelry begins. Perhaps the real tradition of the original Horn Dance is recreated here!

It might be thought that keeping the antlers in the village church would tame their pagan spirit. This was not the experience of 27 year old Jacky Ayre who visited Abbots

10

Bromley with her parents in June 1988. Her father was keen to see the antlers, but the church door seemed to be locked. However when they made enquiries, they were told that this could not be; the church was definitely open. They went back and tried again and found that this time the door opened easily.

Once inside, Jacky's parents went straight over to view the antlers but Jacky was amazed to find herself transfixed. In her own words, 'I couldn't move without great effort, and felt very strange and uneasy. The feeling grew to intense discomfort.'

Forcing herself to move, Jacky left the church and immediately felt better. She decided to walk round the outside of the church, but encountered a pocket of freezing cold air. Again she was most surprised; it was a hot summer day and everywhere else the temperature was in the high 70s.

A few years later, Jacky and her parents returned to Abbots Bromley, this time to watch the famous Horn Dance. Jacky decided to take the opportunity to check out her previous experience. She went back to the church, which this time – on the day of the Horn Dance – was packed with visitors. Jacky writes, '... but I felt the same horrible feelings as before, and again I had to leave'. She has no idea why this should have happened to her, and has so far been unable to discover whether other people have experienced the same thing. Could it be that 'the most primitive dance in Europe' has maintained its power down the centuries and has an aura or a resonance that some people can feel?

ADMASTON

The Ghosts of Blithfield Hall

BLITHFIELD HALL, the ancestral home of the Bagot family, boasts no fewer than five ghosts. Two are male, two female and there is one whose gender is uncertain. This ghost manifests itself as the sound of rustling clothing passing along the lower gallery, and is usually heard in the hour before midnight. It is possibly the swishing of a lady's skirts, but is thought more likely to be the sound of a priest's robes. One room off the gallery is certainly known as the Priest's Room and is believed to have been used by a priest who sought sanctuary at the Hall.

One ghost is referred to as the Grey Lady of Blithfield and has been seen on innumerable occasions in various parts of the building. She wears a lacy cap, a long grey gown, and shoes with shining silver buckles. At her waist, she carries a bunch of keys on a leather thong. She may have been a member of the Bagot family, or possibly a housekeeper.

The other female ghost has been observed in less detail, and is said to disappear when anyone approaches. She wears a cape over a long dress.

The fourth Blithfield ghost was seen by a cleaner and her daughter in 1973. He was in the drawing-room and wore dark clothing. He was seen at three o'clock in the afternoon, and there was plenty of daylight for the two ladies to observe that he was gazing at the floor in an abstracted manner. They also noticed that he wore an unusually shaped ring on his left hand, which he continually rubbed with the fingers of his right hand.

The fifth ghost is seen and heard in the archery ground and is the consequence of a tragic accident that occurred in the 18th century, when a small child fell into a deep well. A gardener attempted to reach the child, but he was an elderly man and he slipped. As he fell, hitting the chains all the way down, his terrified screams echoed up the shaft. Although the well has been filled in long since, the shape of an old man is still seen disappearing into the ground where the well once stood. Even more macabre are the screams heard coming from beneath the ground at the same spot.

ALTON

The Gipsy Ghost at Alton Towers

IN 1847-8 Dr F. A. Paley was living at Alton Towers, the home of the Earl of Shrewsbury. He was the tutor to Bertram, the earl's nephew and heir. At that time the premier earldom of England was Roman Catholic, and it was important to John, the 16th Earl, that Bertram should inherit the title and later pass it down to his own heirs. Bertram was the last Catholic in the family, the next in line to the earldom being distant Protestant cousins.

One evening, Dr Paley and Bertram were riding home at dusk. They were about a mile from Alton Towers, at a spot with a canal on one side and a steep bank thickly set with trees on the other. Dr Paley caught sight of a gipsy woman gazing at them from behind an oak tree, her head bent forward and her face plainly visible. He pointed her out to his pupil, and Bertram spotted her too, quite distinctly.

As the place was very isolated, Dr Paley was intrigued by the woman's presence and decided to investigate further. He dismounted and passed the reins of his horse to Bertram. He set off to climb 20 yards or so up the steep bank to where he'd seen the gipsy woman, intending to question her. When he got to the spot, he was very surprised to find no one there.

Clambering back down to the road, he again checked with Bertram that they really had seen her. The boy was absolutely certain that they had, adding that she was wearing some kind of handkerchief over her head.

When the incident was related to Lady Shrewsbury, she instantly lost all the colour from her face, and was obviously extremely disturbed. She went to her room, and declined to appear at dinner that evening. The family chaplain took Dr Paley on one side and reprimanded him for having inadvertently caused alarm to the family. Dr Paley had been unaware of a family tradition that the apparition of a gipsy woman always preceded the death of an heir. He tried to dismiss it from his mind, since his pupil looked so healthy, but was forced to consider it again when Bertram died of consumption in 1852 and the title passed out of the Catholic line. Dr Paley set out the whole story in a letter he wrote in 1883 to the historian Sir Charles Oman of Oxford University.

The Chained Oak

ANOTHER 'death-in-the-family' legend explains why the great oak tree in the grounds of Alton Towers has strong iron chains wound round its branches. In the late 18th century the Earl of Shrewsbury sent out invitations to members of all the noble families of Europe to attend a grand ball at the newly extended Alton Towers. The surrounding lanes were filled with the carriages of many aristocratic guests driving towards the Towers, as well as dozens of acrobats and jugglers, musicians and dancing bears, who were to provide the entertainment at the ball.

It was a splendid occasion. The earl welcomed his guests and the revelries began. Suddenly, half-way through the evening, the music faltered to a stop and everyone ceased dancing. All eyes were drawn to an old man who shuffled his way to the centre of the room. His grey hair was long and unkempt and his clothes were ragged and dirty. His eyes, however, were remarkably blue and piercing. No one could imagine how he had managed to get into the house without being stopped by the servants.

The earl strode up to this uninvited guest and demanded to know what he meant by interrupting the festivities. The old man replied that he was a travelling fortune-teller, and that he hoped the earl would let him earn a bite to eat by telling the fortunes of the guests. The earl snorted with derision and ordered his servants to seize the old man and eject him from the estate. As the interloper was hustled from the room, the guests began to mock and jeer, but they grew silent as the fortune-teller began to shout a warning at the earl. The laughter died away as they heard him prophesy that every time a branch fell from the great oak in the grounds, a member of the earl's family would die. The old man pulled himself away from the hands of the earl's men and walked out by himself.

Although the party resumed and the guests dismissed the foolish old man from their thoughts, the earl could not forget his prophetic words so easily. The next day, after the guests had all departed, he went out into the grounds and stared thoughtfully at the great oak beside the drive. Decisively, he strode away and ordered the gardeners to wind strong iron chains around the branches so that none of them could ever fall. The chains used were so strong and numerous that the earl could rest easy in the knowledge that the branches were permanently secure. Visitors to Alton Towers will see that the great oak is still there and still bound in its chains.

A similar legend was attached to the cedar of Lebanon tree, planted in 1677 at Bretby Park. Again the tree was wound in chains, because of a belief that a branch falling would presage a death in the family living in Bretby Hall. This legend took on new and exotic ramifications when Lord Carnarvon, a former owner of Bretby Hall, helped to open the tomb of Tutankhamun in Egypt in 1922. It was widely held that the curse of the Pharaohs would fall on those who had disturbed Tutankhamun's tomb, and Lord Carnarvon died the following year. Hundreds flocked to Bretby Park in 1923 to find that a branch of the cedar had indeed broken at the time of his death, and was hanging in the chains. This legendary tree was felled in 1953.

The Ghost in the Ladies Loo

MARGARET BUCKLE, known affectionately to everyone on the estate as 'Mrs B', had worked at Alton Towers for over 12 years before she saw the ghost in 1978. For four or five weeks she had thought that someone was playing tricks on her as she worked in the toilet building. She would be cleaning the wash basins when she would hear the outside door bang, then one of the toilet cubicle doors would close. Each time, Mrs B would call out, 'Good morning!' but would receive no reply. She decided that one of her colleagues was playing a joke on her, and she was determined to catch them at it.

The next time it happened, as she shouted, 'Good morning', she whirled round to confront her tormenter. However, as usual there was no one there. Margaret carried on with her cleaning but suddenly she felt extremely cold, even though it was a pleasant warm day. She turned again and there before her she saw a figure wearing a black cloak, a floppy, big-brimmed black hat, and pointed toe boots with small black buttons up the side. In her own words, Mrs B 'took one look then ran like mad, nearly knocking over my boss, Mr Noaks'.

When she had recovered enough to be able to talk, Margaret told him what she'd seen, and was told not to worry as the ghost wouldn't hurt her. When she saw the ghost again, six weeks later, she shouted at it, 'Keep away from me. I'm not responsible for turning Alton Towers into what it is today!' The events occurred shortly after the stately home had begun to be developed into a leisure theme park with white-knuckle rides, pirate ships and fast-food restaurants. Mrs B believes that the cloaked figure might be a ghost from the past who does not approve of the changes.

Although Mrs B couldn't tell whether her ghostly visitor

was male or female, she had a feeling that it was a lady. Other staff have since seen her in the gift shop and near the Swiss Cottage in the gardens, and the ghost is often blamed for moving objects around. Visitors to Alton Towers have seen her by the moat, and some have even felt an invisible hand trying to push them off the low wall that borders the moat.

One theory is that she is the ghost of a young woman of high birth who was planning to run away with a young man of whom her family did not approve. The planned elopement was discovered and her father seized the young couple as they were about to ride off on horseback. He locked the girl in a tower, but she tried to escape by climbing through the tiny window. Tragically, she fell and was drowned in the moat. Most of the staff believe that she is the lady who appears dressed in her 19th century riding clothes, just as she was on the night of her failed elopement.

ANSLOW

Kit-Mark of the Burnt Gate

OLGA and Tony Eaton moved into the Burnt Gate pub in 1967, and Olga immediately felt uneasy in the part of the building that is now the pub lounge, and the room above it. 'I've never seen anything myself,' she says, 'but I've always sensed a presence of some kind.'

Her son Jonathan was four at the time, and as soon as they moved into the Burnt Gate, he began to see and talk with an invisible friend. He told his family that the friend was a boy named 'Kit-Mark', which struck Olga as a very unusual name, well outside the everyday experience of her son. When Jonathan acted as a page-boy at a wedding, he

17

looked at himself in the mirror and told his mother that he was dressed 'just like Kit-Mark'. On another occasion, he pointed to a picture of a 17th century drummer-boy in a Ladybird book and remarked that it *was* Kit-Mark.

Jonathan's conversations with Kit-Mark continued for many years, the drummer-boy appearing to him at the top of the garden and in his bedroom, sometimes even sitting on his bed. Jonathan's sister Julia was born a year after the family came to the Burnt Gate. Although she grew up with her brother talking about Kit-Mark, she was 19 before she first saw him. One night in 1987 she came downstairs and went through the lounge. In a corner of the room she saw a pale figure sitting in front of a mirror. It was a blond-haired boy of about 15, entirely dressed in white. 'He had a very sad face,' Julia told me, 'but he wasn't in the least frightening.' She saw the boy several other times in the room above the lounge, and every time she sensed a sad feeling coming from him.

The unusual name of Burnt Gate is almost certainly explained by the fact that the building was originally a keeper's cottage standing at the gate to the part of Needwood Forest called Brende Wood. The Burnt Gate must have begun its life as the Brende Gate.

BAGNALL

Old Ma Hatton with the Evil Eye

IN the 17th century an old couple named Hatton lived in what was then the isolated village of Bagnall. The fact that the old woman had a squint was enough to convince the villagers that she possessed the Evil Eye, and could cause illness or even death in both cattle and men simply by looking at them.

As if the old woman's squint wasn't proof enough, her husband was prone on occasion to running into the woods at night, making strange animal noises. The villagers would see him shrieking and whistling, with his wife hurrying after him, calling for him to return. There was no doubt in anyone's mind that they both must be witches.

Most of the Bagnall people kept away from Ma Hatton and her husband, but whenever a child took ill, or some money was lost, they knew that the Hattons had caused it. When a cow belonging to Joseph Cope stopped giving milk, Joe had no doubt that Ma Hatton had 'overlooked' the animal, glanced at it in passing, and given it the Evil Eye.

Joseph Cope armed himself with an axe, and with four of his cronies went to the Hattons' cottage. He took with him the afflicted cow. Trying not to look directly into Ma Hatton's eyes, he ordered her to revoke the evil spell.

Under threat of being hit with the axe, the old woman called down God's blessing on the animal and the men grudgingly allowed her to go back into her home. When the cow recovered a few days later and began to give milk again, everyone in the village knew that the witch Ma Hatton had cured it just as magically as she had blighted it in the first place!

BASFORD GREEN

Horsley's Stone

THE story behind Horsley's Stone is a Cain-and-Abel tale of two bachelor brothers who both fell in love with their young housekeeper. The elder one slew his younger brother, and threw his body into the river Coombe. To prevent the crime being discovered, he then pushed a massive rocking stone from its precarious position over the steep bank, down into the Coombe Valley, covering the body.

The ghost of the dead brother returned in the form of a bird, which would sit on the stone and sing its plaintive and haunting song. Many residents of nearby Basford Green and Ipstones have heard the bird, and say that its song is so sad and moving that they have to fight back their tears. They tell of one young lad who loved to poach fish from the Coombe. He had no fear of the gamekeeper, but he did dread Horsley's ghost. One night as he fished by lantern light, the bird flew into the lantern and put out the light. It then perched on Horsley's Stone and sang its usual haunting melody. The terrified poacher fled, and never poached in the Coombe Valley locality again.

An even older story about Horsley's Stone is that captives of battle used to be executed on it during the Dark Ages.

At the beginning of the century, a land-owner decided to cut up the 13 ton Horsley's Stone to use it for building. However the masons he employed were terrified of its history, and only managed to cut one piece away before refusing to continue. Perhaps a little bird sang to them. The result is that Horsley's Stone remains in Coombe Valley, a monument to either the terrible ancient executions, or to the fratricide of the Horsley brother from whom it gets its name.

BILSTON

On the Other Hand

IN 1780 the coal miners of Bilston were being terrorised by an evil spirit which haunted their pit, and they decided to seek the help of White Rabbit, a well-known local male white witch. He cast a spell to protect the men, and advised them to exorcise the spirit at midnight. They should walk through the pit, led by a miner carrying a Bible in his right hand. They should begin by chanting the Lord's Prayer backwards, then recite, 'Matthew, Mark, Luke and John, God bless the errand that we're on'.

The miners did as they were bid, entering the mine at midnight, reciting the words they'd been told, and their leader carrying the Bible in his hand. Suddenly the evil spirit appeared before them. The leader held the Bible aloft, and the men's chanting grew louder and more fervent. The evil spirit seemed unimpressed and moved slowly towards them!

Then one of the miners spotted what was wrong. 'Caggy, yer fool!' he cried. 'The book's in yer wrong 'ond.'

Caggy quickly passed the Bible from his left hand to his right, and the spirit shrieked and disappeared, leaving nothing but a faint trace of smoke and a smell of brimstone.

The Night of the Dead

THREE HUNDRED years before Guy Fawkes and the Gunpowder Plot, the people of Bilston used to celebrate 5th November with lighted candles and a procession. It was the eve of St Leonard's Day, their patron saint, and the townspeople would carry the lighted candles into the church graveyard, and spend the night keeping vigil over the dead. The vigil was known as the Wakes.

Later the custom was secularised and moved to the Market Place. The Wakes became a three-day carnival with bare knuckle fighting, bear baiting, cock fighting and above all continuous drinking of gin, wine, porter and ale! The Wakes was outlawed by the authorities in the late 18th century, but the festival was revived in the 1930s when it was moved from November to June.

BLOXWICH

The Ghost of Wallington Heath

WALLINGTON HOUSE, the home of the Russell family, was sold in 1904 and became the Convent of St Paul of Chartres. However, in the 18th century it was a coaching inn called the King's Arms, and the ghost that still haunts it dates back to a wild winter's night in the 1720s.

A blizzard was blowing, and the stage coaches could go no further because the road was blocked with high snow drifts. All the coaches were parked on the heath, and the passengers were lodged at the King's Arms, while the coachmen and postillions were put up in the cottages opposite. Among the travellers was a young woman travelling alone, and carrying a roll of French silk. Like all the others she went to bed early that night, in order to make an early start the next day. The gale howled all night, but most of the exhausted passengers slept soundly.

Next day everyone was up at daybreak, except the young lady. At breakfast, among all the throng of the extra guests the young lady's absence was not really noticed. It was only when the passengers took their seats on the coach that people realised that the lady with the roll of silk was not there.

A search was made, and her mutilated body was discovered in an upper room. It was obvious that she had been foully murdered. Further investigations proved that her roll of silk had disappeared. Also missing was one of the ostlers and one of the landlord's horses. It was realised that the sounds of her brutal murder had been masked by the noise of the storm.

Legend has it that the girl's spirit refuses to leave the King's Arms, and over the years many people have seen her on wild windy nights sitting under the ash tree opposite the inn, quietly weeping. One passer-by saw her on a stormy night in February 1993.

Moreover, her silhouette appears outlined on the inside wall of the inn; no matter how often the wall is painted or replastered, the figure still shows through. Gordon Varley now lives in Great Wyrley but he grew up in Bloxwich. He tells me that older Bloxwich people still remember their parents hurrying past the spot, or even refusing to venture that way at all.

BLURTON

An Unlucky Talisman

WHEN Stephen Morris found a small metal object on the road near his home in 1983 he thought he would clean it up and use it as an interesting ornament. It was about six inches high, and shaped like an anchor with a circle joined to the bottom of it. When his girlfriend Janet saw it she took an instant dislike to it and asked Stephen to throw it away. Since she had no rational explanation for her feelings, Stephen ignored her advice and hung the object on the wall.

That night he went to bed at eleven o'clock, but woke up sweating. The whole room was shaking and there was a deafening noise. He could hear his dog Patch barking. Very scared, he got out of bed and switched on the light. He was amazed that everything looked normal. He opened the bedroom door and saw that Patch was fast asleep. He even looked outside but nothing seemed to be out of place.

As he returned to his bedroom, however, he noticed that the anchor on the wall was slanting, as were all his pictures. Had there been a minor earth tremor? The next day, Stephen asked the residents of the neighbouring flats whether they had heard any disturbance during the night, but no one had heard anything. When he told Janet about the incident, she again advised him to get rid of his new ornament, but he just laughed.

A few weeks later, he moved the object to the living-room, hanging it above the fireplace. One night, after a late night out, a friend called Alan stayed at Stephen's flat, sleeping in the living-room. When Alan woke next morning, everything was soaking wet, including his clothes and hair. At first, Stephen thought that his friend was playing a practical joke but soon realised that he wasn't. The only rational answer seemed to be some kind of leak, but when he called in the Water Board they could find nothing wrong and were unable to explain the wetness.

It was at this point that Stephen decided to take the object down and put it in a drawer, but when he moved to a bigger house he again displayed it on his wall. His life entered a difficult patch; he split up with his girlfriend, started drinking, and in his own words, 'I could see my life being in ruins'. He came to the conclusion that his 'lucky' anchor was not helping at all. He took it to an old mine shaft and threw it in. After this decisive action, Stephen's life began to improve and no further strange events have occurred.

The notion that objects can bring good or bad luck is an old one. Writing in 1937, the Revd Frank Brighton describes how charms of various kinds have always been used by inhabitants of north Staffordshire. Bits of brass, copper, lead and other metals with strange letters scratched on them would be placed on churns 'to make the butter come quicker and more plentiful'. Families going on a journey would put on similar talismans as a protection against accidents. A girl who had been jilted would throw twelve smooth stones into a pool of water, one at a time, to bring her lover back to her. Farmers would attach to a scythe handle or to a plough a small piece of parchment, known as a bee, to improve their work rate. And the selling of love charms, designed to attract the affections of a particular girl or boy, provided a steady source of income for many old women of the moorlands area.

So Stephen Morris, in hanging up his lucky talisman, even though it proved in the end to be a bad luck charm, was following a very ancient tradition of this area.

BURNTWOOD

Hide-and-Seek with a Ghost

IN 1934, when Ivan Vinnell was twelve, he and a group of friends had been playing a long range game of hide-and-seek one evening. He and one companion became fed up as they had seen nothing of the others for some time. The two boys decided to make their way slowly and quietly along the road to their base on the local green. When they saw a figure emerge from the thick hedge on their right, their immediate thought was that they'd been spotted.

However, the figure proved to be a very tall man, accompanied by a dog which looked black in the half-moonlight. He walked across the road right in front of them, then passed through the hedge on their left. 'It wasn't an illusion, because we *both* saw it at the *same time*,' Ivan emphasises. The two boys returned to the spot in the full light of the next day, but neither of them could work out how the man and dog could have passed through the dense hedges.

When Ivan left school, he went to work in Lichfield and therefore had to use this road every day. He admits that he always felt a sense of unease when he reached the spot where he'd seen the ghostly figure, though he never saw it again.

However Ivan later told his uncle about the incident. He was amazed when his uncle told him that, as a young man, he'd seen the same figure with the dog several times! On the first occasion, the man had passed close to him. He'd been so scared that he'd struck out with his walking stick, only to find that his stick had passed right through the figure. Needless to say, this did nothing to allay his fears. He subsequently saw the ghost on several occasions, and Ivan has met other older residents of the area who also say that they have encountered exactly the same figure.

The location of the sightings has always been the same, on the road from Woodhouses to Burntwood, close to Burntwood Hospital. Ivan is now 72, but his memory of the ghostly figure is as vivid as the night he saw it 60 years ago. 'There is a row of lime trees on the left,' he reports, 'and a holly tree on the right.' He calculates that sightings of the ghost go back at least 100 years.

BURSLEM

Molly Leigh: the Hamil Witch

IF you lived in the Hamil area of Burslem at the beginning of the 18th century, young Molly Leigh was a girl to be wary of. She was then about 15 years old, but was already a strong-willed and difficult girl. People said that she could 'bend anyone and anything to her will'. She had no scruples about cheating people when she sold produce, frequently selling watered milk. Moreover she refused to attend church.

Everyone was afraid of Molly. She had strange wild eyes, and people said that if she stared at a child she could cause it to become ill. If anyone upset her, those weird eyes would also cause cattle belonging to the offender to become lame. She had, in fact, the power of the Evil Eye.

As she grew older, she preferred her own company to that of friends and neighbours. Her only companion was a black raven that perched on her shoulder whenever she went out. People noticed that this familiar would sit on the roof and watch them if they walked by her cottage, and everyone believed that it then told Molly who was passing.

It was also thought significant that the hawthorn bush by her cottage never came into bloom. What went on inside the cottage was unknown, since no neighbour ever dared to enter. However, they were sure that she had dealings with the devil, entering into pacts in exchange for her supernatural gifts.

On one occasion, the Revd Thomas Spencer tried unsuccessfully to shoot Molly's raven. He spent the next three weeks in sheer agony, unable to walk. The villagers concluded that Parson Spencer had incurred Molly's wrath.

While her company was avoided by all and sundry, most residents of the locality regarded her with a mixture of awe, fear and respect. They knew she was a witch but, after all, she was *their* witch. In this way, Molly Leigh lived out her solitary life for 63 years.

In March 1748 Molly died. She was buried in St John's churchyard by Parson Spencer on 1st April. Because she was a witch, her grave was dug north to south, at right-angles to all the other graves.

After the burial, the parson and the mourners went first to the Turk's Head to fortify themselves with hot punch, then they set off across Jackfield towards Molly's cottage. They intended to 'purify' the witch's home by means of prayer and hymn-singing. When they arrived at the gloomy cottage, the mourners hung back for the parson to enter first. He hesitated, then flung open the door and strode in.

Seconds later, he raced out and fled back towards the Turk's Head, followed by the curious villagers. Safely ensconced in the tavern, Parson Spencer took another drink and informed the others that as he had crossed Molly's threshold he had seen her there, sitting by her fire! Their imaginations ran riot. They had been willing to put up with a witch among them when she was alive, but the notion of a dead witch among them was terrifying.

As Molly was obviously too much for one parson to cope with, it was decided that he should call in three more vicars from Stoke, Newchapel and Wolstanton. The four clergymen agreed on a plan of action. At midnight on the following Sunday, they approached Molly's grave, chanting prayers as they did so. They ordered the sexton who accompanied them to dig up the witch's coffin, then climbed down into the grave to examine it, but were startled by a hoarse croak. They looked up to see a raven perched on the rim of the hole.

Convinced that this was Molly's familiar come to watch what they were doing, they panicked and ran away. However, before he fled, Parson Spencer managed to grab hold of the raven with one hand and lift the lid of the coffin with the other. He threw the fluttering bird inside, let the lid drop again, and scuttled after his fellow-preachers.

Later the four men found the courage to return to Molly's cottage where they prayed that the witch's ghost should leave the Hamil area for ever. They may not have been completely successful as sightings of the Hamil witch recurred throughout the 18th and 19th centuries. She was often heard singing, 'Weight and measure sold I never, Milk and water sold I ever.'

Eighty year old Mrs Eaton, whose family has always lived in the Hamil area, tells me that she was always afraid of Molly's ghost as a girl. She believed the other children's tales about the witch, until her father told her that his great-grandmother claimed she could remember Molly Leigh. Mrs Eaton's family have always insisted that Molly was not a witch, although they admit her appearance was rough and witch-like. She discounts the tale about Molly's black raven being entombed with her, though she does fully accept the story of her ghost being seen in the cottage after her burial. The tradition in Mrs Eaton's family was that the villagers piled extra stones on Molly's tomb to keep her spirit in. She thinks that the witch legend is due to the superstitious nature of the Burslem people of the 18th and 19th centuries.

Not everyone agrees with Mrs Eaton's assessment of Molly. Even into the 20th century, Burslem miners would not go down the pit if they met a cross-eyed woman on their way to work. They would not take the risk, just in case the lady with strange eyes was in fact the ghost of Molly Leigh, the Hamil witch. Mr K. Booth of Hanley tells me that Molly's ghost still haunts the area, appearing to a friend of his whose bedroom overlooks the churchyard.

BURTON-UPON-TRENT

The Ghost that Followed the Landlord

THE haunted Royal Oak public house is in Burton's Market Place, close to St Modwen's church. 'Billy Banks' became the licensee of the pub in 1978, and in May he moved in with his wife, his ten year old son and his daughter aged eight. Immediately, Bill was aware of a strange atmosphere about the place, and heard unexplained noises from empty rooms. Lights that were definitely switched off at night were found by a passing policeman to be on again at three o'clock in the morning.

Soon after the Banks family had moved in, Bill had some friends from Belper over to stay. The pub was rather full and the friends had to sleep in the living-room. Bill was very surprised when he came down next morning to find that the friends were all dressed and packed. 'Don't take it personally, Bill,' they told him, 'but we're going home and we're never coming back.' They went on to explain that they had been awake all night, convinced that there was someone else with them in the room.

Bill's mother only came up from Kent to see him twice during the seven years he was at the Royal Oak. 'We're really fond of each other,' Bill told me, 'but she absolutely hated the place.'

While he was landlord there, everything in Bill's life went badly wrong, including his marriage. 'Although I somehow knew that the presence could not hurt me physically, I felt that it was disturbing me mentally and psychologically,' he told me. 'I'm not one for organised religion,' he added, 'but I do believe in Good and Evil and there was a battle going on there.'

In 1985 Bill moved to another Burton pub with his second wife, thinking that he had left the ghosts behind him and could start a new life. However, it was not to be. One evening at about 10.45 pm, everyone in the pub lounge stopped talking and stared at the ceiling. From the upstairs room came a tremendous sound of banging and bumping, as if furniture was being thrown about. Bill thought that his 15 year old daughter must be somehow causing the row, and called up to her to stop. Getting no reply, he hurried upstairs to find all the furniture in its proper place and his daughter fast asleep. 'She was genuinely asleep,' he recalls. 'I would have known if she were pretending.' Bill also checked in the room of his 15 year old step-daughter, but she too was fast asleep. He is still not sure whether the strange phenomenon at the second pub was caused by the presence of two adolescent girls, or whether the ghosts of the Royal Oak had moved to the new pub with him.

Apparently, something of the Royal Oak's ghosts still remained and several subsequent publicans have been frightened away. There have been five or six landlords in the nine years since Bill left, and at least one had to seek help and advice from a local priest. Bill Banks has now left the pub trade and is coming to terms with his previous disturbed life. To preserve his privacy I have not used Bill's real name.

CAULDON LOWE

The Fairies of Cauldon Lowe

> 'And where have you been, my Mary,
> And where have you been from me?'
> 'I've been to the top of the Cauldon Lowe
> The midsummer night to see.'

CAULDON LOWE, or Caldonlow as it is sometimes spelt, is the name of both a village and a nearby hill. When poet Mary Howitt wrote her ballad *The Fairies Of The Cauldon Lowe* in 1847, she based it on an old legend that the hill was inhabited by a race of fairies. Given the date of her poem, it is not surprising that her fairies are dainty little creatures, innocent and entirely benign.

The ballad tells how the girl Mary spends midsummer night on the hill observing 100 fairies dancing to the music of nine harpists. After their dance, the good fairies spend the rest of the night doing kind deeds to help the humans down below. They send water to help the mill-wheel turn, winds to blow mildew from the widow's corn, lint seed to grow flax in the weaver's croft. A bearded brownie spins a little sheet for Mary's bed and an apron for her mother.

Had Mary Howitt written the poem a decade or two later, the fairies would have sported gossamer wings and carried wands, because such was the idealised view of the later Victorians. However, if she had written it much earlier, then the fairies would have been very different. The older image of fairies was that they were very dangerous. It was unlucky to refer to them directly as fairies, much safer to call them the Hidden People or the Little People. To refer to them by the name of fairies was unsafe enough, but if you actually saw one you could be struck blind.

Traditionally they were ugly creatures, who stole human babies from their cots because the fairy race needed to

31

interbreed with humans to survive. When fairies stole a baby, they would leave a changeling in its place. This might be hideously ugly, certainly it would be strange-looking, and occasionally the changeling would be a life-less wooden doll.

One tradition states that fairies were an ancient race who inhabited Britain before the invading Celts drove them out; another says that they are the descendants of pre-Christian gods and goddesses who lived in the streams and trees. The question of their size is interesting. Originally they were the same size as humans or even bigger. By the Middle Ages, it was thought that the fairy aristocrats were tall and elegant, but the lower orders were less beautiful and were no bigger than a three year old child. This differ-ence in beauty between the nobility and the lower classes obviously reflects the social structure of the time. The notion that all fairies were miniature creatures came in much later, and was an attempt to explain why they were difficult to spot. Similarly, their butterfly wings explained how they travelled quickly and how they entered houses without being seen.

The dangerous fairies who lived in the Peak District often inhabited the many burial mounds known as Lows or Lowes. Cauldon Lowe is just one example of a village where a burial mound adds a Low to the name. There are many more: Warslow, Wardlow, Grindlow and Bleaklow are just a few. Tales of these mound-dwelling fairies include stories that they ate human flesh, though these legends may have resulted from the discovery of the human remains buried there.

'There's a Man in the Room!'

WHEN Mark and Margaret Mellor bought a house in Cauldon Lowe, Mark had no idea that 23 West Fields would turn out to be haunted. It was a new house, built where some back-to-back houses had been demolished.

It was the early hours of a summer night in 1989 when

something woke Mark up. He was surprised to find the room unusually light. He saw a figure standing by the bed and assumed it was Margaret.

A few seconds later Margaret woke and saw the figure. She of course assumed it was her husband and asked him, 'What's the matter?' As she asked him the question, her left hand brushed against Mark still lying beside her. Realising that figure couldn't possibly be him, she screamed.

As they both sat up and looked at the figure, it vanished! They now thought that there was an intruder, possibly a burglar, inside the house. Mark got up immediately and searched the whole house but found nothing, and there was no sign of any break-in. Whoever the visitor was, he wasn't an intruder of the living kind. Mark is convinced he saw a ghost that night.

CHEADLE

Old Ammy

JOSEPH AMBROSE PIERCE is buried in Cheadle cemetery, but his ghost, known affectionately as Old Ammy, often visits his former home to warn its present occupants when danger is coming. One person who saw the ghost was Patrick Allen, who with his mother was staying with his great-grandmother while she was ill. During the night, he saw Old Ammy come into his room and pull up the blankets to cover him. Although the actions were kind and gentle, Michael was nevertheless worried to see this stranger in the house.

When he told his mother about the incident and described the old man, she reassured him by saying, 'Don't worry. It's only Old Ammy'. She was concerned however, as sometimes the visit of the ghost presaged a death, and her grandmother was ill. However, a few days later, her cousin was buried alive in a mining disaster at Foxfield colliery near Dilhorne, and he was very, very lucky to be rescued. She decided that this may have been what caused Old Ammy's appearance on that occasion.

When she was a girl, Mrs Allen used to stay with her grandmother. She asked her about the ghost of Old Ammy, and was told that Old Ammy had never harmed anyone when he was alive, and his ghost wouldn't harm anyone now he was dead.

Nevertheless, his appearances were disturbing because of the events that always followed them. Two of his visits took place immediately before the death of both of Mrs Allen's parents. A spiritualist medium was called in to try to discover why Ammy's spirit was tied to the house. The medium held a seance, and told the family that there was something in the house that Ammy was searching for. She confirmed what they had already deduced, namely that he would not do harm to any of them.

Mrs Allen recalls one occasion in 1944 when, as a young married woman with a husband in the Forces, she was staying with her grandmother. It was a cold February night, and she was in bed lying with her knees up, looking at the ceiling. Suddenly she heard the purring of a cat. This was puzzling as the bedroom door was shut tight, and in any case her grandmother didn't have any cats. There was a sudden weight on her chest as if the cat had jumped on her. As it seemed to walk down the length of her body, all the strength went out of her. She could not move at all. In her own words, she 'couldn't even bend her little finger'. At the same time, she heard the most ear-splitting noises like hundreds of steam engines roaring past. The weight on her body reached her legs, then went away.

She was convinced that a cat had been on the bed and that it must still be in the room. Jumping out of bed, she searched the place, looking under the bed, in the wardrobe, in every nook and cranny. There was no cat, and the bedroom door was still firmly shut. When she consulted her grandmother, the old lady stated firmly that it was definitely a visit from Old Ammy. They wondered what this visit might foretell, and were concerned that it might be death. A week later, Mrs Allen received news that her husband had been killed in action in Burma.

CHECKLEY

Mrs Hutchinson of the Rectory

MRS HUTCHINSON, the widow of the Revd William Hutchinson, was known as a bit of a tartar during her life; her ghost has continued in the same vein since her death in 1895.

A widow since 1878, Mrs Hutchinson kept a stern and unsmiling eye on village proceedings, causing most of the villagers to regard her with nervous trepidation. Should any family fail to attend church on a Sunday, they knew that Mrs Hutchinson would be calling to demand their reasons, and to admonish them if the reasons were not compelling enough. She ruled the parish with a rod of iron. She had a particular loathing of two carefree young ladies who liked to ride their horses through the churchyard, and throughout her life Mrs Hutchinson made her disapproving attitude about them very plain.

Death does not seem to have dimmed her vigilance. When the Revd Ralph Phillips moved into the rectory in the 1940s, he gave a house-warming party. Mrs Hutchinson turned up too! After the party, some of the guests were sleeping at the rectory. One had retired to bed when he noticed that his room had no clock. He decided to go downstairs to fetch a watch from his coat pocket. As he returned he met on the stairs an old lady with a disapproving expression. Assuming that she too was a guest, he wished her a good-night but received no acknowledgement in return.

At breakfast, he looked around but could see no sign of the old lady. He asked his host if there were any more guests but was told there were not. When he described the old lady as wearing a long black frock and a white mob cap, and mentioned her walking stick, Ralph Phillips told him that undoubtedly he had met the formidable Mrs Hutchinson!

Ralph and his wife saw the same figure many times during their time at the rectory, and on one occasion Mrs Phillips heard her name being called while she was alone in the house. In the rectory, a meeting of the parish council was interrupted by repeated knocking on the door, said to have been caused by the ghost of Mrs Hutchinson. No doubt she disapproved of some item on the agenda.

Mrs Hutchinson does not restrict her haunting to the rectory, however. In 1939 she was seen at the Hutchinson Memorial School by the headmistress, Miss Hilda Stonehouse. When Miss Stonehouse saw an old lady walking across the playground wearing a grey dress, mob cap and waistcoat, she assumed that it was someone visiting her housekeeper, Mrs Pillans. However, she was surprised when the housekeeper was adamant that she had received no visitors that day. A few days later, Miss Stonehouse was at the rectory and saw on the wall a painting of the same lady who had crossed the playground. It was a portrait of Mrs Hutchinson.

Hooded Monks and Little White Dogs

THERE has always been a problem in getting men to dig graves in Checkley churchyard, due to widespread stories that people who venture there feel a disturbing sense of being watched. Passers-by will take care not to walk through the churchyard, for the same reason. One who took no heed of its reputation was the headmistress Hilda Stonehouse who featured in the preceding piece. She used to cut through the churchyard almost every day to reach

36

the school house, and she knew the path well. However one night when she attempted to cross it in the dark, she felt something impede her progress. She just could not proceed any further. It was as if she had come to a tree or a brick wall across the path, though she knew full well that she had not. Although she could not see any physical obstruction, she was unable to continue and was forced to retrace her steps to the church, then walk home via the road.

Miss Stonehouse loved to play the organ in Checkley church, and the rector allowed her to do so whenever she wished. When she had finished playing she would turn off the lights, then feel her way to the north door, lock it, then take the key to the rectory. She was never afraid of being in the darkened church, but on several occasions she saw a hooded figure near the altar. The then rector told Hilda that he too had seen the same phantom. Other people who have seen the figure there include the postmistress who used to arrange flowers in church and her daughter-in-law.

The figure resembles a robed monk with a cowl, and is said to be the ghost of Thomas Chawney, the last Abbot of Croxden, whose abbey was despoiled at the time of the Dissolution and given into the hands of 'a dissolute adventurer' named Geoffrey Foljambe. Since the abbot's grave in the chancel of Checkley church lies alongside those of the Foljambe family, it has been suggested that the abbot finds the company uncongenial. However, no one who has seen the hooded monk has felt any fear of it. All have sensed it to be a very friendly presence.

Another of Checkley's ghosts is that of a little white dog seen in and around the rectory. One lady who saw it pass through a wall in the entrance hall fled and refused to go near the building again, but most people find this apparition intriguing rather than frightening.

COBRIDGE

The Screaming White Rabbit

IN the 1850s travellers were very wary of taking the path from Cobridge to Etruria, especially at night. The problem lay in the spot called The Grove, widely believed to be haunted. Passers-by would first hear a piercing scream, like that of a young boy in terror. They would then see a large rabbit 'as white as milk' jump out from the trees by the path. It would run along the path, unafraid of anyone it met, then instantly disappear.

One brave nocturnal traveller decided that he would catch the rabbit. He took the same route several nights in succession, until he heard the screaming sound. He waited and, as he had anticipated, the white rabbit appeared, coming down the track towards him. It drew level with him and he attempted to seize it. However, his hands passed clean through the rabbit, leaving him in a shocked condition and suffering with a dislocated shoulder.

The legend about the white rabbit began in August 1833, when two boys, 14 year old John Holdcroft and 16 year old Charles Shaw, were at The Grove playing pitch and toss. Charles was losing to his younger companion, and when he had lost all his money, he grew angry and accused John of cheating. The quarrel escalated into a fight, and Charles seized John by the throat, choking him to death. Alarmed at what he had done, Charles Shaw tied a rope round the neck of his victim, then hung the body from the branch of a tree, hoping to make it look as if John had committed suicide. The body was not found for some months, and Charles found he could not keep his terrible secret to himself. He confessed to the murder, and was tried at Burslem in March 1834. He was sentenced to death, but this was later commuted to transportation.

Soon after this, the legend about The Grove being

haunted started. The screaming sound is said to be the death screams of young John Holdcroft, and the mysterious white rabbit is his restless spirit.

COVEN

A White-Haired Lady in a Flowery Apron

WHEN Audrey Blount and her husband bought a primitive wood and asbestos bungalow in 1959, I wonder whether the name of their village gave them cause to expect any strange phenomena? The name of the bungalow, 'Sunny Croft', was pleasant enough, and it was in Lawn Lane which sounds fine. But the village was called Coven!

Soon after they moved in, they began to hear heavy footsteps on the gravel path outside, every morning at seven o'clock. At first, Mr Blount would rush outside, only to find no one there and the gate shut. After a while he gave up bothering. Audrey says that they learned to ignore the sounds, treating them as an everyday part of their life, although on one occasion the footsteps, sounding like a man wearing heavy boots, went on all night and kept Audrey awake.

One morning when Audrey was cleaning the windows, she suddenly 'saw' an image of a little old lady with white hair in a bun, and for some reason she 'knew' that the old lady was the last person to clean those windows. A little later, her three year old daughter Linda said, 'Mum, who was that old lady looking at the roses with you in the garden?' Linda went on to describe a small, plump lady in a flowery apron, with white hair 'done up in a sort of lump on her head'. It was obviously the same lady.

Then a friend, Mrs Rowlands, told Audrey that she'd seen the same lady in the dining-room of Sunny Croft, while another friend, Mrs Stephens, said quite separately and independently that she'd received a mental picture of the same white-haired lady.

Audrey knew that the original owners of the bungalow were a Mr and Mrs Lawrence. She decided to try to find someone who had known them, and went to see a Mrs Berry who lived lower down Lawn Lane. She confirmed to Audrey that the description of the plump lady with her white hair in a bun was an exact description of the bungalow's former owner. Now that Audrey knew for certain who her ghost was, she asked Mrs Stephens, who was a member of a Spiritualist church, to pray for Mrs Lawrence. She did so, and the ghostly phenomena ceased.

ELFORD

A Statue Carved in Mist

THE ghost that appeared to the Revd Francis Paget in the mid 19th century inspired in him awe, but no sense of fear. Francis was the rector at Elford, three miles north of Tamworth, and he was held in great respect by the village. His son became the village squire and lived in Elford Hall, adjacent to the rectory. The Hall was demolished in 1966 but the rectory, now a private house, still stands.

In a letter written in 1877 Francis Paget describes how, several years before, he had left his study early one winter afternoon and was walking along a passage that ran the whole length of the rectory. As he approached the living-room door at the end of the passage, he was surprised to see that it appeared obscured in mist. This area was always well lit by a wide window facing south, and although the weather outside was slightly foggy, the mist by the door inside the house seemed much denser. Francis later described the mist as similar to a jet of steam exposed to cold air.

As Francis approached, the mist gathered into one spot and deepened until it took the form of a human figure. The head and shoulders were quite distinct, although the lower part seemed to be clothed in a full length robe or cloak. The cloak reached the flagstoned floor, and was very wide at the bottom so that the whole shape was a long pyramid. The light through the window fell clearly on the figure before him, and the rector observed that he could see the panels of the door through the lower part of the robe, where the misty vapour seemed thinner. He describes what he saw as 'completely colourless – a statue carved in mist'.

He stood transfixed. He did not at this stage regard what he could see as anything supernatural, but as a unique and wonderful effect of the light from the window, an unusual but natural phenomenon. But as he watched, the figure turned its head and he recognised the face of a very close friend. The expression on the features was peaceful and kind, and not in the least frightening. The mist-figure gave Francis a look of deep affection, and suddenly all the mist had cleared.

The rector was amazed and in awe of what he had seen, but had no sense of fear. He walked forward to where the figure had been, opened the door, and went into the room to where his meal was set.

The next day, he received news that his friend had died peacefully at the time that he had seen the mist. He had no idea that his friend was near death, he had not heard from him for some weeks, and he had not been thinking about him on the day that the apparition appeared.

It seemed to the rector that his friend had come to him of his own volition to say goodbye. In his letter, Francis Paget recorded that since that day, every time he passed the spot where he had encountered 'the statue carved in mist' he remembered his friend with a feeling of great awe and deep affection.

ENDON

Well-Dressing: a Christianised Pagan Rite

ALTHOUGH Derbyshire is the home of well-dressing, with almost 50 villages boasting their own festivals, a very small number occur outside that county. The one at Endon, between Leek and Stoke-on-Trent, is one of that number.

Well-dressing, once known as well-flowering, is the art of decorating wells and springs with pictures made from flowers, moss, leaves, seeds and other natural substances. Originally, well-dressing was part of pagan worship, a tribute to water spirits or nymphs. Floral offerings were made to ensure that water continued to flow. It was a recognition of the essential part that water plays in human existence, a tangible expression of respect for a vital element. An added attraction was that water from the wells had magic curative properties.

The early Christian Church tried to stamp out this expression of the older religion, but later came to realise that the customs could be retained and Christianised. The wells were renamed with the names of saints replacing those of spirits and goddesses.

The 1993 Endon well-dressing took place at the end of May during the Spring Bank Holiday, and lasted for three days, beginning with a church service on the Saturday afternoon. The custom was revived in 1845 and has been celebrated every year since. It includes the coronation of a Well-Dressing Queen. She is actually crowned four times; twice on the Saturday and twice more on the Monday!

The Monday festival includes a fair, where Morris dancers play a part, as well as a competition of Tossing the Hay. In this, the competitors use a pitchfork to toss a sack of hay over a horizontal pole, though originally a sheaf of hay was pitched. The Endon Well-Dressing is a good example of how Christian elements, including the Saturday church service, combine with older pagan dances and rural games.

GRINDON

The Headless Horseman

THE headless horseman gallops the length and breadth of the Manifold Valley, terrifying all who see him. As well as Grindon, he has been seen in or near the villages of Onecote, Butterton and Wetton. The witness who saw him near Grindon in the mid 19th century gave a detailed description of the horseman and his mount.

The headless man wore shining golden armour which glowed like fire. His flowing cloak, which covered the haunches of the horse, was also gold in colour. He was carrying a short staff in his right hand. His horse was white, and appeared to be frozen in a galloping position with both its fore and hind legs extended.

The Leek man who saw him at a crossroads near Onecote in 1935 was a little less romantic in his description, stating that it was 'a man on an 'orse without a yed, an awful gory sight!'

The farmer who was returning from Leek two centuries earlier was somewhat the worse for drink, and accepted a lift on the man's horse. It wasn't until he was mounted behind the stranger, that he noticed that his kind helper was headless! The nightmare ride which followed, over heath and moor, through ditches and stone walls, left the foolish farmer so bruised and battered that he died a few days later.

A man from Butterton was riding home when the headless horseman joined him, riding alongside. The man's horse trembled with fear and his dog howled in terror.

Although the horseman disappeared before they reached the village, both the horse and dog died the next day.

As to the headless horseman's identity, there are several versions of the legend to pick from. The most widely quoted is that he is the ghost of a noted warrior chief from the area, who was killed in a battle against the Scots far away in north Yorkshire. At the time of his decapitation he was carrying his studded staff, the emblem of his authority. After his death, his white horse carried his headless body back to his native county, where he still rides through the darkest nights. It is said that if the horseman points his staff at any witness, then this foretells that a catastrophe will happen to a close relative.

A more mundane explanation is that the ghost is that of a pedlar murdered by savage thieves, who compounded their crime by cutting off the victim's head before setting his headless body to gallop away on his horse, as a brutal practical joke.

A third version tells how seven 16th century clergymen, called out to lay the spirit of the headless horseman, reported back that the ghost was one of four evil spirits cast out of heaven 'to roam over the face of the earth until the crack of doom'. This would make him one of the Four Horsemen of the Apocalypse, referred to in the Book of Revelations. His pale horse would indicate that he was the horseman representing death. Why this legendary figure should restrict himself to patrolling the Manifold Valley is inexplicable.

HANBURY

The Fauld Disaster of 1944

SHOULD you ever walk up to the crater just half a mile east of Hanbury, you may well wish to take a companion or two. Even in company, the spot is desolate and lonely. Solitary visitors have reported the location too unhappy to bear for more than a few minutes. One told me that she had heard strange discordant singing in the air, while another told of putting his ear to the ground and hearing an eerie keening sound from below.

The disaster that occurred here in 1944 went unreported in the media for this was wartime, and the censor would not permit the news to be broadcast. Ammunition and bombs were stored in the disused tunnels under Fauld Gypsum mines. At just after eleven o'clock on the morning of Monday 27th November 1944, 3,000 tons of explosives suddenly detonated. To call the result a devastation would be an understatement. It was the largest single explosion of the war, prior to the atom bombs dropped on Hiroshima and Nagasaki.

At Fauld, 81 people died. Two nearby woods and Upper Hayes Farm disappeared, while Hanbury Fields Farm was buried under the debris. It is estimated that a million tons of earth were thrown up to eleven miles in the air. A reservoir burst, causing 15 ft of mud to flood into Fauld plaster works. Pieces of dead cattle littered the whole area. Most buildings in Hanbury suffered damage, houses in Tutbury had their roofs shattered, and two church steeples in Burton-on-Trent were severely cracked. The explosion was heard 35 miles away in Coventry and Leicester, and was seismographically recorded in Geneva and in Rome. The crater that resulted from the Fauld explosion was 800 ft long and 120 ft deep.

And yet it could have been even worse. A second, much larger ammunition store, which was connected to the first by a narrow tunnel, did not explode. If it had, then much of east Staffordshire would have been wiped from the map.

The villagers of Hanbury and Fauld still treat the spot with reverence and respect, and many of them find it difficult to talk about the event of 50 years ago. Visitors feel that it carries an atmosphere of desolation. Even visitors who know little of its history have commented on their feelings of overwhelming grief when they stand there. No one has explained the singing sounds in the air or the underground weeping heard by a few visitors, but all report the sense of loss that haunts the area round the Fauld crater.

HANFORD

A Grey Shape and a Musty Smell

VICKY EVITT has always been conscious of a strange atmosphere in the front room of her house in Hanford since moving in ten years ago. There was a disturbing feeling of being watched accompanied by a musty, almost fishy, smell. The house is an otherwise normal detached one, built in the 1920s.

One night, as she was walking from the bathroom to the bedroom, she saw a grey shape in front of her. It looked quite tangible, but when Vicky put out her hands to touch it, there was nothing there. She says that her feelings about this inexplicable event are those of curiosity, not of fear.

Vicky's 22 year old son Robin has taken a photograph of the garden. When the picture was developed, the family were amazed to find that the same grey shape could be seen standing on top of the garden steps.

Then, in late 1993, Robin was writing up a report on his visit to a stone circle site. He is a keen student of stone circles and the rituals that were once enacted there. It was about 10 pm when Robin became aware of the musty smell, and had a feeling that some invisible presence was standing behind him. Suddenly, their cat shot off the chair and ran from the room. Robin admits that the hairs on the back of his neck were standing on edge by this time. He telephoned a friend who is interested in psychic phenomena and she advised him to leave the house for a while.

Robin decided to follow her advice and went for a walk. When he returned, the room – and the cat – were back to normal.

He now wonders whether the subject he was studying, the rituals associated with stone circle sites, could have triggered the events of that night.

HARTSHILL

The Craft Shop

WHEN John and Maria bought a shop in Hartshill, with the intention of turning it into a craft centre, they were certainly not expecting that things would be entirely problem-free. There was a lot of work to be done on renovating and altering the premises, just for starters.

However, there was no way they could have anticipated just how terrifying their life was about to become. The first indication happened within a week of moving in, when Maria woke to the sound of hammering coming from downstairs. The sounds ceased after a few minutes, but she woke John, who went to investigate. He found the room below as he had left it, completely bare, with a hammer and a few other tools lying on the concrete floor. The hammering was repeated every night, and the couple mentioned it to a neighbour. He told them that he had often complained to the previous owner about night-time hammering. They decided to leave the tools in another part of the house, and this seemed to cure the problem.

The next chapter in the mystery occurred when John, his father and Maria were working in rooms at the back of the building. John's mother came in and asked who the man was working in the front of the shop. 'There's no one else here but us,' was John's puzzled reply, but his mother insisted that she had glanced into the shop window as she'd passed in the street and seen a man there. John unlocked the door that led into the shop and checked. There was no one there, the street door was locked and bolted and all the windows were secure.

Eventually, the work was completed and the craft shop opened. It became something of a meeting place for actors from The Vic theatre, as well as other people who were interested in arts and crafts. One morning, a young woman came into their living-room, and immediately said that she felt there was something strange there. She pointed to a corner of the room and said that there was something about it that frightened her. That afternoon, a male friend came in and said that he too was uneasy about the same spot. He had no idea that anyone else had commented on it earlier that day. Over the weeks, other callers reported a similar reaction to the room. John had heard scratching noises coming from the corner of the room, but had thought that it was probably due to mice in the wall cavity.

So far, John and Maria had experienced a series of incidents that were puzzling but not really scary. The next two events were far more intense. As John was lying in bed one night, he had an overpowering sensation that there was someone or something moving about the room. It was pitch black and he could see nothing, but in some strange way he knew exactly where the presence was moving: past the window and towards the wardrobe. Although he was initially petrified, he forced himself to get out of bed and switch on the light. He saw that Maria had her eyes open, and she was shaking with fear. 'Thank God you've put the light on,' she gasped. 'I've just had the most horrible feeling there was something in the room!' She went on to describe how she had experienced the exact same feeling that John had, even to the path taken by the presence.

The final phenomenon was discovered when they went downstairs into their living-room. There, in the very hard-wearing carpet tiles, were a number of deep white scratches. The marks were pointing towards the centre of the room and formed a perfect circle. John tried every way

48

to find out how the scratch marks could have been made in the virtually indestructible tiles. He found that he could not mark the tiles with a knife or even a chisel. It was inexplicable. The scratches stayed in place for the rest of their time at the craft shop, but when they later moved to Scotland they took the carpet tiles with them. When they unloaded them and began to relay them, they were amazed to discover that all the scratch marks had disappeared.

The Ghost of Hartshill Hospital

IN 1991, Ian Brown was in Hartshill Orthopaedic hospital, a resident of Pavilion Ward Three. He'd had a leg amputated, but had recovered enough to be able to get about. He always liked to be the first into the hospital bathroom every morning, so he would make his way there before the lights came on.

This particular morning he was having a wash in the bathroom at about six o'clock, when he heard someone behind him say, 'Are you all right?' He recalls that it was a lady's voice, which he describes as being 'nice and soft'. As he had only one leg, Ian held on to the basin, and strained his neck and eyes to look towards the door. He saw a lady he hadn't seen before. She had a greyish face and Ian thought how old she was to be a nurse. In answer to her question he replied, 'Yes, thank you,' and carried on washing.

Later that day, Ian asked one of the nurses who the old lady was, but she did not know. Shortly after this, two nurses came and asked him what he had seen. When he described the lady, they told him he had seen the hospital ghost. They were rather surprised as until then this ghost had been seen by many of the staff but never by a patient. The two nurses told Ian that one male nurse had been petrified by the sight of the old lady. When his colleagues found him, they described him as having his eyes 'popping out of his head'.

Ian Brown found it hard to settle in bed that night, but comforted himself by reasoning that the ghost must be harmless. After all, if she had wanted to harm him, she could have done so quite easily when he was alone in the bathroom. Once he was calmer, he decided that when he saw her again, he would ask her who she was, and why she was there. He was very disappointed that he never met her again during his stay in the hospital, but believes that she still visits the nursing staff there.

HATHERTON

The Skull Goblet

WHEN the ghost of Sir Hugh de Hatherton returned to Hatherton Hall one Christmas Eve in the mid 19th century, he was seeking what was rightfully his. A party was taking place, with vintage port being served from a rather special drinking vessel: a goblet made from a human skull, lined with silver! The guests all found this a great novelty, and swore that wine had never tasted as fine as it did from the skull.

They saw no harm in drinking the health of the original owner of the skull. Lord Hatherton had earlier explained to those present that the skull was part of a skeleton dug up where a private chapel once stood, the remains of one of his ancestors. Since the skull had become detached, he had had it lined with silver and made into a unique drinking goblet.

As the clock struck twelve, the company heard approaching footsteps and grew silent. As they did so, the goblet began to spin until it fell to the floor. At the same moment a headless figure in armour appeared in the room. He bowed to those present, crossed the room and walked away through the closed door. No one was in any doubt that it was Sir Hugh.

Their deductions were confirmed when they realised that the skull goblet had disappeared. The next day, the whole house was searched but there was still no sign of it. However, on the frosty lawn outside, they found a silver ball. It was made of rolled up silver plate, the lining of the goblet.

Lord Hatherton concluded that while Sir Hugh regarded the skull as his rightful property, his knightly ancestor had no intention of taking the silver which did not belong to him.

HEDNESFORD

The Skeleton Tree

MARY SHERWOOD of Hednesford was very much in love with her young man, Richard Gordon, but he had one fault that both distressed and alarmed her. He loved to go out poaching on Cannock Chase at night. He was skillful in all the arts of poaching, and he revelled in the excitement of evading the attempts of the rangers and keepers to catch him.

However Mary was a pretty and determined girl, and in order to win her, Richard had to promise to give up the poacher's craft. The young couple did most of their wooing out on Cannock Chase, beneath the shade of a green and leafy oak tree. Although Mary's parents were initially opposed to the match, they were impressed when he swore to give up his nocturnal habits, and eventually they gave their consent.

The wedding was arranged, and just like young men today, the groom arranged for a night out drinking with his friends, his last night as a bachelor. Many of his friends were fellow-poachers and they teased Richard unmercifully about his promise to give up his old ways. 'He's under the thumb already!' they jeered. After a few more drinks, Richard decided that his promise would really begin when he was married. Tonight he was still free, he thought, and maybe his friends were right when they said that he should spend one last night on Cannock Chase, enjoying his favourite pursuit.

Despite the wild and stormy weather, off they went for a night's poaching, stopping to make their plans under the very tree where Richard had promised Mary that he would never poach again. His keen hearing and quick wits were somewhat fuddled with drink however, and he failed to hear the stealthy approach of a ranger. The man overheard enough to know what they were up to, and he stepped out and challenged them.

The poachers yelled their defiance, the ranger became angry, and then someone drew a gun. One shot was fired and the ranger fell dead. As Richard bent over the man to see if he could help, his erstwhile friends fled. Other keepers ran up to find Richard Gordon alone with the dead man. He was taken, tried and hanged.

On the morning after his arrest, Mary walked forlornly to the tree where she had spent happy hours with her lover. It was completely bare of leaves, a dead skeleton of a tree. During the days leading up to Richard's trial, Mary would wander the Chase talking to herself, and singing. She even took to sleeping on the ground under the skeleton tree. She had lost her wits, everyone said.

Finally, on the day her lover was hanged, Mary walked down to a pool of clear water and, as the prison bell tolled, she drowned herself in it. The skeleton tree never grew leaves again, and it has stood there for 250 years, a stark memorial to the hanged poacher and his drowned lover.

HOPWAS

The Ghost that Only Children can See

THE village of Hopwas, situated between Tamworth and Lichfield, has two graveyards. One is attached to St Chad's church on Hopwas Hill, but this only dates from 1881. There is a much older one in Hints Road where there was once a mission church, St John's. It is this older cemetery that is said to be haunted by the ghost of a young boy. One strange facet of this haunting is that the ghost is only seen by children.

In the spring of 1982, the members of the village Women's Institute undertook a survey of the headstones in the two churchyards, registering their positions and dates, and taking rubbings of the words. They wished to make a permanent record of the words on the gravestones that would still remain, even when time and the weather had erased the actual carved inscriptions.

The ladies were very careful not to disturb the tombstones, though when working in St John's graveyard they found it necessary to pull back weeds and ivy in order to trace some of the names. One of the headstones was that of a boy who died on 15th March 1878 at the age of six.

In the same week as the WI survey, Pat Waugh was walking past St John's churchyard with her three year old son Neil in a pushchair. As they passed the gateway, Neil looked into the churchyard and said, 'Look, Mummy, a little boy in there'. Pat looked for herself but saw no one. Her son repeated, 'A little boy over there,' and pointed to the left-hand corner of the cemetery towards the boy's grave. Pat checked again but there was definitely nobody present. She walked on and thought no more about it.

However, the next day she was talking to her friend Glenda Smith who lives about 20 yards from the St John's cemetery. During the conversation, Glen mentioned a

53

strange thing that her daughter Becky had said the evening before. They had been sitting in the lounge, which had a window facing the pavement that passes the graveyard. Suddenly Becky had looked up and exclaimed that there was a little boy at the window. Glen could see nothing there, but her daughter had been insistent that a boy was still looking in their window. Of course, when Pat told Glen that her son had also claimed to see a little boy that day, a boy that Pat couldn't see, the two women found the two events 'too much of a coincidence' and rather disturbing.

When Pat and Glen told the other WI members, they too were a little alarmed. Rosemary Vanstone wondered whether they had disturbed the headstone while making a rubbing of it. Others wondered whether the fact that it was springtime when the boy had died might have some connection with his appearing in the spring of 1982.

However, it may be that ghost had been appearing long before Hopwas WI did their survey. Talking recently to a man who has lived in the village all his life, I learned that the local children have always talked about St John's graveyard being haunted. 'We always hurried past there,' he recalled. 'It wasn't a place we wanted to hang about!'

Of course, it is easy to dismiss a haunting that only children can see, and put it down to childish imagination. On the other hand, it is known that children can sense things that adults have learned to filter out, to dismiss as non-rational. And it is worth bearing in mind that both Neil and Becky told their parents that they could see the boy on the same day, in the same area, and quite independently of each other.

ILAM

Good Company

IN a lonely cottage in the hills high above Ilam there once lived an old woman. She had a small garden with its own spring, and she was able to grow a few herbs, a wild dog-rose, and a gooseberry bush. She always counted her blessings, for her cottage had a stout door and a roof that kept out the rain. She kept the place clean and tidy, and a neighbouring farmer would occasionally remember to bring her some turves for the fire. He also gave her clean straw for her bed, and his wife had once given the old woman a quilt. With a roof over her head, a fire, and a warm bed to sleep in, there was nothing the old woman could possibly wish for.

Except company. Someone to talk to.

When the farmer came by, it was always a fleeting visit as he was keen to get back to his work. Once she saw a tinker with a rabbit in each hand, but he was being pursued by a gamekeeper, and neither of them were able to stop and keep her company.

So she made the best of it; she was grateful for what she did have and banished her yearning for company from her mind.

One day the farmer did call for a few minutes. He had come to bring her some more turves, but while he was there he passed on the local gossip about the big house in the village. He told her that the old squire had died and his nephew had come up from London to be the new squire. All the old servants were refusing to work for him as he had 'turned out the luck'.

For hundreds of years, milk and bread had been left out every night, for the little people. This new young squire would have none of it! He'd given the milk to his dogs and had thrown the bread to them. Little people indeed!

None of the old servants would stay to work for a master who didn't respect the little people, and new servants from London were coming to take over their duties.

The farmer was in a hurry to get on to the neighbouring village where the annual well-dressings were being prepared, so he departed after imparting his news. The old woman was left alone again. She would have liked to dress her own spring but she didn't have enough petals from her solitary dog-rose. She sighed but then set to work briskly, sweeping her floor clean. She had intended to bake a flat oatcake, but the turves were too wet to catch fire. That night as she lay in bed, she heard a plaintive voice outside her door, crying, 'Oh dear oh, where can I go in rain and snow?'

'Who's out there?' the woman called out bravely.

The thin voice came again. 'Oh dear oh, what can I do? Let me come in and stay with you.'

It might be a ghost, the old woman thought. Or even ... But the poor thing must be wet through and miserable, whatever it is. 'Come in and welcome,' she shouted. She saw a thin brown hand creep round the door and something small slipped into the cottage. 'If you can find a warm spot, you're welcome to sleep in it,' she told it. 'Though the fire's too damp to burn and the oatcake is not cooked.'

She fell asleep again, but in the night she woke to find her fire flaming brightly, and her oatcake baking with a delicious smell, and a new pile of dry turves stacked neatly in the corner. Without looking directly at her visitor, for she knew you must never look at a hob, the woman rose. She poured two mugs of milk and broke the oatcake in half. She ate her share, and left the rest for her visitor.

The next morning she woke, but her helper had disappeared. When she went out into her garden, she could not believe her eyes. There were piles of flower petals everywhere; crimson and gold, pink and white, blue and yellow.

Joyfully, she set to work, spreading wet clay on the flat rock next to the spring, then pressing the flower petals into it. As she worked, she had the feeling that her night-time visitor came back to help her, though again she did not look directly at him. Just as she finished, she heard voices and looked up to see the farmer with a number of people on his cart. He explained that these were the well judges on their way to the village, and that he'd brought them this way so that she would see people for a few minutes that day. The judges alighted from the cart and examined the old woman's well-dressing before continuing on their journey into the village.

That evening they were back to tell the old woman that she had won that year's contest. They presented her with three silver pennies, and congratulated her on her wonderful well-dressing.

The farmer whispered that all the flower petals from the squire's garden had mysteriously disappeared overnight. He had been so furious that he was off back to London the next day.

'That's what comes of turning luck away,' he said. 'He should never have refused to leave food out for the little people. It just serves him right.' And from somewhere outside the cottage, they heard a deep chuckle of agreement.

The old woman was happy and contented. She knew that she now had good food, a good fire, and above all, good company.

IPSTONES

Kirkgrim and Padfoot

THE older residents of Ipstones tell how they used to hurry home from school, particularly in the winter, so that they could bring water from the well before darkness fell. It was widely believed that every well had a spirit that guarded it, frightening enough in daylight. To meet it in the dark would be unthinkable.

One of the Ipstones wells was called Indefont. One Ipstones resident, who wishes to be known only as Joe, says that Indefont well was guarded by both a Kirkgrim and a Padfoot. A Padfoot was a spirit that appeared in the shape of a large dog, while a Kirkgrim could take on any shape at all. When Joe was a boy, he knew several men who had seen a big dog sitting by the well. When they had struck at the animal with a stick, the stick had passed clean through the shape, proving that it was either a Padfoot or a Kirkgrim.

The Wandering Jew

STORIES of the Wandering Jew abound in the moorlands area of north Staffordshire. One Sunday in 1658, a lame old man who lived alone in a cottage near Ipstones heard a knock at his door. He answered it, and found a stranger, a Jew strangely dressed in a gown of purple shag. The stranger asked for a cup of beer, and the old man replied that he was welcome to one, but that he would have to get a cup and help himself. The Jew asked how long the man had been lame, and was told that the affliction had come on many years before.

The stranger said that he could cure the lameness, and told the old man to put three leaves of balm into his beer for the next three weeks and he would be made whole. He also told the man to serve God zealously and constantly. The old man obeyed the instructions, and his lameness left him.

There are several versions of the legend to explain who the Wandering Jew was; most of them refer to Jesus making his last journey, carrying his cross to the place of Crucifixion. In one version of the tale, Jesus asked a Jew named Ahasuerus for a drink of water, in another permission to rest in a gateway. In all the versions, the request was refused and as a result, Ahasuerus was condemned to wander the earth down the centuries, until the second coming. The age of the Wandering Jew appears to vary, since every time he attains the age of 100, he returns to the age of 30, as he was at the time of the Crucifixion.

The legend goes on to state that if a stranger asks you for a drink of water or beer, do not refuse or you will suffer ill-fortune. Nor must you ask the age of the stranger; he may look any age between 30 and 100, but in reality he is nearly 2,000 years old!

The Ghosts of the Hermitage

A cutting from a newspaper dated 1916 tells of a 300 year old haunted farmhouse in Ipstones called the Hermitage. The tenant of the Hermitage, Bennett Fallowes, has become rather 'ghost-hardened' over the years, but visitors to the farm are frequently terrified.

Mr Fallowes' brother-in-law Edward Wheeldon admits that the nocturnal sounds of footsteps running up and down the stairs left him with his hair standing on end. A young servant girl became hysterical when she heard unearthly screams from under her window, and Richard Fallowes, a cousin of the tenant, heard music being played on an organ during the night. The most terrified was undoubtedly Miss Jane Fallowes who felt a frozen ghostly hand over her face.

All of these manifestations, plus other unexplained lights and noises heard at the Hermitage, are said to be connected to the ghost of a little old miser who once lived there. However, there is also a ghostly hound, described as being 'as big as a donkey', which has often been seen at the end of the lane. One man who saw the giant dog attempted to kick at it, but his foot went clean through the apparition.

KIDSGROVE

The Strange Manifestations at Old Rode Mill Farm

WHEN Mrs J. Goddard was single, she lived with her parents at Old Rode Mill Farm, a building dating back to the 12th century. As well as a working farm, it had been a paper mill, but was now used for breeding horses. Mrs Goddard does not want me to give her maiden name, so I'll call her Jane Johnson. The farmhouse, situated about three miles north-west of Kidsgrove, had a chequered history, and seemed to have brought bad luck to many people who lived there. Previous residents had failed in business, or had encountered problems in their personal life. These bouts of misfortune seemed to occur at three-yearly intervals, and Jane reports that her own parents' marriage broke up while they were there.

In 1987 Jane was 21 years old. Early one morning, she woke suddenly and found that her bed was shaking violently. She was sleeping on her front but managed to turn and look up. Although it was still dark, she saw a white shape on the corner of her bed. When I asked her if it was like a person, she was unable to be certain. 'It was a white vision,' she said, 'stretching from the corner of my bed to the ceiling.'

About three weeks later, Jane was again woken by the violent shaking of the bed. This time it was even more alarming as she was unable to move. She was wide awake, but felt pinned face down in her bed. She then felt a cold hand moving across her shoulders! The incident was ended by an almighty crash. 'It sounded as if someone had thrown a heavy book down on to a table,' Jane told me.

The crash seemed to break her paralysis, and Jane found she could now move. She got out of bed but could find no source for the crashing sound.

She recalls that when she lived at the farm, she also heard frequent creaking from the floor-boards on the landing outside her bedroom. Her dogs and cats would refuse to cross the landing too.

After her experiences, a local vicar agreed to come to the farm. Although she hadn't told him where the strange events had taken place, he went straight to her room and gazed at the corner of her bed where she had seen her 'white vision'. He seemed to know just where it had happened, Jane says, and he said prayers in her room, to bless it.

She was unable to find any explanation for the phenomena she experienced, although she was told that victims of the English Civil War had been buried locally. Another possible source of the haunting is a gravestone that stands in the garden. It has no words or markings on it, and Jane does not know whether it marks a human grave or the resting place of an animal, but she wonders whether it could have some connection with the bizarre manifestations she encountered there.

KINVER

The Ghost of Billy Howe

THE ghost that haunts the area around the Stewponey Hotel in Kinver is said to be that of a murderous footpad named William Howe. Betty Lloyd saw him in February 1957, and reported that he wore a tricorn hat and carried a brace of long-barrelled pistols in his hands. A policeman, who prefers to be named only as Jack, saw the same figure in 1972. Again the three-cornered hat was noticed, though on this occasion the pistols were not seen.

Local people claim that the ghost is definitely that of

Billy Howe, who was tried and hanged in 1813 for the murder of a local farmer, Benjamin Robins of Dunsley Hall. Howe was a notorious thief, like a highwayman on foot, who used to hold up and rob wealthy travellers. The killing of Benjamin Robins took place during one of Howe's hold-ups, close to the Stewponey Hotel, on a dark snowy night in 1812.

William Howe, a native of Stourbridge, was found guilty and hanged. Afterwards, his body was sent back to Kinver for gibbeting; this meant that it was put in a metal cage and displayed near the scene of his crime until the flesh had rotted from his bones. In a similar case in Leicestershire, the body of an executed murderer was gibbeted for 20 years before being taken down and buried! In the early years of this century a skeleton was dug up in Gibbet Wood, and this was believed to be that of the footpad Billy Howe.

LEEK

The Witch and the Oatcake

IN the early 17th century, an old lady lived in Gettliffe's Yard, off Derby Street. She lived with her cat, and her neighbours suspected her of being a witch. They noticed that their baking always failed to turn out satisfactorily when the cat came near them.

On one occasion, one neighbour was cooking oatcakes, a north Staffordshire delicacy still enjoyed to this day. When she saw the cat lurking nearby, she threw a sizzling hot oatcake at it. The oatcake hit the animal, causing it to flee back inside the old lady's house. The neighbour called her friends and they cautiously approached the house. They could hear the cat screeching inside, but when they entered they found that it was the old witch who was howling in pain. They were sure that their suspicions were justified when they saw why she was howling. She was in pain from a severe burn on her back caused, they were convinced, by the hot oatcake.

To See the Sun Set Twice

IN Leek, it is possible to gain yourself twelve months worth of good fortune, lasting from one midsummer to the next. You need to visit the churchyard of St Edward the Confessor on the 20th, 22nd or 23rd of June, and to stand in the part known as Doctors' Corner, where the graves of eight doctors are situated. If the weather is fine, all you have to do is to look west towards the rocky hills called the Roaches. It is unlikely that you will be alone, because people come from all over the world to be in that spot at midsummer, and to watch a unique natural phenomenon.

After watching the sun set behind the hill called Bosley Cloud, you should wait patiently. Your fellow watchers will hold their collective breath until the sun unsets itself! It slowly reappears from behind Bosley Cloud, only to set again over the Cheshire plain.

This rare double sunset only happens on these three days of the year, and can only be observed from the vantage point of Doctors' Corner in St Edward's churchyard. Those who are privileged to see it can count themselves doubly lucky, because the year that follows will bring them good fortune in both love and business affairs.

Ghosts of Brough Park

IN 1972 Alan Woodcock and a friend were walking through Brough Park from the bandstand towards St Edward's church. Alan heard a sound which he thought sounded like a large dog choking on a chain. Although it was 8.30 pm and getting dark, he could see the silhouette of a man and a dog some way ahead, not far from the churchyard. The man and dog were walking towards Alan and his friend, but when they were quite near they simply faded away. Alan couldn't believe his eyes and checked with his friend, and he too had seen the man and dog slowly disappear.

An hour later Alan was relating the incident to a Mr Harry Stanway. When Mr Stanway heard that Alan had seen a ghost in Brough Park, he interrupted the story. 'Was it the Roman soldier?' he asked. On being told that it wasn't, he continued, 'Ah, then it would be the man with a dog'. He told Alan that these particular ghosts had been seen many times and that they always come down the slope from the churchyard, then fade away. He himself had seen them 20 years earlier.

The ghost that Roger Turner met on a Wednesday afternoon in June 1993 was more substantial than a fading shadow and, it must be said, more attractive! Roger was on an ancient cobbled footpath known as Dickie's Gutter, which runs steeply downhill from St Edward's church and the Garden of Remembrance towards Brough Park. It is shaded by overhanging trees, and is close to the area called Petit France. Roger was indulging in his favourite hobby of searching for coins with the aid of a metal detector, and he admits he was keeping a watchful eye out for the park-keeper 'or any other nosey parkers'.

He was searching by the edge of the path by St Edward's churchyard when his ear-drums were blasted by a signal from his headset. Expecting nothing more than a modern coin, though hoping for something like a bun-head penny, Roger was thrilled to discover a silver 1933 half-crown. He was just about to clean the soil off the coin, when he looked up and saw 'the most fascinating-looking girl I have ever set eyes on!'

She was sitting on the ground with her back to the old sandstone wall that runs on the side of the path, and had a dark, gipsy-like appearance, with long coiled black hair down to her waist. She was wearing a dress of black chiffon lace with dazzling white cuffs and collar. Her knees were drawn up and her fingers were interlocked round them. Her knee-length boots were cross-laced with eyelets and hooks. She sat, staring wide-eyed straight at Roger for some five or six seconds.

Thinking he had better give her an explanation about his metal detector, and what he was doing there, he opened his mouth but found that he was unable to speak. Moreover, his legs wouldn't allow him to move. He says that he felt as if he were wearing iron boots and standing over an electro-magnet. Suddenly, his precious silver coin fell from his fingers, and he stooped to pick it up. He shivered as the temperature seemed to plummet, and when he glanced up again the girl had gone 'like a dream in the night'.

Roger is ex-RAF, and was trained by the SAS, and says that he is not easily frightened. He pulled himself together and walked to the spot where the girl had been sitting. The only trace that she had ever been there was a heady rose-scented perfume. And, of course, he still had his 1933 silver half-crown, a tangible reminder of the strange events of that summer afternoon.

A Victorian Figure in the Cemetery

ANOTHER ghost from a past era was seen one summer a few years ago by Susan Critchlow in the town cemetery. This was not the church graveyard mentioned earlier, but the cemetery off the Cheadle Road. She was walking along Wardle Road towards Selbourne Road, when she glanced towards the cemetery. She saw the stationary figure of a man, standing on a slightly raised bank by a clump of trees. The way he was dressed caught her attention. He had on a long black cloak and a tall black hat, as if he came from the Victorian era. She watched him for a minute or so, then carried on home.

Susan saw the same man again about a year later. This time she was with her twin sister and her elder brother, walking towards The Herdsman public house by way of the old railway line that runs alongside the cattle market.

Susan was with her brother, her sister was some way ahead. This time the figure, wearing the same tall hat and the long black cloak, was standing on some ground recently incorporated into the cemetery. Again he was perfectly still, and staring straight at Susan and her brother. By the time they had climbed from the railway line and were alongside The Herdsman, the figure had disappeared. On this occasion her brother also saw the man, although her sister had seen nothing.

LICHFIELD

Field of the Dead

ETYMOLOGISTS disagree about the origin of the name of Lichfield. Some scholars claim it means 'Field near Letocetum', a Roman settlement about a mile from the present site of Lichfield. Others say it means either 'Field of the Marsh' or 'Field of the Dead'. The latter derivation refers to the legend of three Saxon chiefs who were slain here during the reign of the Roman emperor Diocletian towards the end of the 4th century.

The Roman empire, which had once ruled the whole of the known world, was beginning to crumble, and Diocletian needed someone to blame. The early Christian Church made a useful scapegoat. The Roman emperor ordered his soldiers to wipe out any signs of Christianity, to slay its followers without mercy and to burn their villages. When Diocletian came to Britain, he undertook the task of wiping out the new faith with enthusiasm.

The three Saxon chiefs, sometimes referred to as three kings, were adherents of the new faith and they decided to make a stand. They assembled their tiny army of ill-clad men, armed only with clubs, reaping hooks and a few broken swords. They advanced on the much larger force of well-equipped and well-trained Roman soldiers and fought a brave but futile battle. In less than an hour, the entire Saxon force was slain.

Diocletian ordered all the bodies, including the three chiefs, to be heaped into a huge pile and then set on fire. The names of most of the dead are unknown, as is usually the case, but a rhyme names the three 'kings' as Cope, Borrow and Hill. The site of their funeral pyre became known as Lichfield, the Field of the Dead. In the year 700, a cathedral was built on the site of the pyre, the first in the kingdom of Mercia. The present Lichfield cathedral is unique in having three spires; which are a fortuitous reminder of the three Saxon kings. The three dead kings are also to be seen on the Lichfield coat of arms.

Elspeth Trapped in a Tunnel

THE ghost of a 13 year old girl who died trapped in a sub-terranean tunnel beneath the streets of Lichfield, has been seen in two local shops. Roger Emsley, who owns a pet shop in Sandford Street, thinks that he disturbed the ghost when he was reorganising his cellar. Over the years he has got used to sudden dramatic drops in temperature, and to the mysterious movement of stock that occurs while the shop is unoccupied. Both Roger and his son have observed moving shadows. His two dogs now refuse to go anywhere near the cellar, whereas they were once quite happy to sleep there. The sudden difference in their behaviour has occurred since the afternoon when they came yelping and howling up the cellar steps.

In the cellar is the entrance to an old tunnel which is thought to have once led to Lichfield cathedral. The tunnel was blocked up many years ago, and Roger thinks that the strange phenomena in his pet shop are connected to the legend of a young girl who was lost in the tunnel at the time it was sealed.

In a furniture shop in nearby Bird Street, the ghostly

figure of a young girl has been seen on at least two separate occasions. In 1986 a terrified carpet fitter fled the shop, after catching sight of a girl watching him in the empty shop. According to the shop owner, Christopher Whitehouse, the fitter was a down-to-earth man and not easily terrified, but he refused to work alone in the shop again.

In 1991 a cleaner called Ann was vacuuming an upstairs showroom at the furniture shop when she noticed the sudden icy drop in temperature. She turned round and saw a misty vapour appearing behind one of the chairs. It formed the upper half of a young girl of about 13 years of age, wearing a grey shawl and a bonnet. She had a thin dirty face, and her wispy hair was ginger in colour. Her sad expression moved Ann almost to tears. Ann 'heard' a plaintive voice inside her head, which told her that the girl's name was Elspeth and that the room Ann was cleaning had once been hers.

Ann knew nothing of the carpet fitter's fright, five years earlier, and had never heard the legend of the little girl trapped in the tunnel, but she is now convinced that Elspeth is that girl. Ann is horrified to think that Elspeth's body must still lie trapped in the tunnel beneath the streets of Lichfield.

Ghosts at the King's Head

BIRD STREET is also the location of the King's Head Hotel, the scene of several ghostly appearances. One is the ghost of a lovely young girl who met her death in a tragic fire there. She has been seen in the function room on several occasions by the daughter of the present landlord, Graham Kennett.

Another ghost is that of a former licensee whose name was George. He appears in the cellar where he died. Mr Kennett confirms that, even today, the cellar does have an indefinable but definite eerie atmosphere.

However, the most famous spectre is that of the laughing Cavalier. He met his death outside in the street when he fought a courageous but losing sword-fight with a number of Cromwellian soldiers. After being hacked to death, his body was dragged down to the cellars of the King's Head and left there. His ghost, still bearing wounds, but now in good spirits and with a laughing expression, has been seen both in the hotel and wandering the streets of Lichfield. He is completely oblivious of the modern traffic and of pedestrians, passing through them, with a permanent smile on his face.

LONGNOR

Driven from His Home

THE strange phenomena which were experienced by Mr Wood and his cousin in a cottage in Longnor hit the national press. They also succeeded in driving Mr Wood from his home. Mr Wood had returned to the cottage after a stay in hospital, during which his elderly mother had died. In the early hours of 15th January 1960 he woke with the feeling that his own hand was being held by another, which was icy and invisible. He told himself that he was being silly, and that his imagination was playing tricks on him. Eventually he went back to sleep.

Over the next few nights, his sleep was disturbed by peculiar metallic noises, which he described as being like the sound of the handle of an iron bucket. Then one night a tremendous crash woke him. Convinced that a ceiling had collapsed in another bedroom, Mr Wood went to investigate but could not find the cause. The next morning he checked again, but all the rooms looked perfectly normal. An alarmed Mr Wood decided to spend a few days with friends in Leek. They tried to convince him that the strange events were all in his imagination.

When he returned to his cottage in Longnor, things appeared to have quietened down until a few weeks later when he heard what sounded like objects bumping on the stairs. When he checked he found that a number of empty cartons had indeed been thrown down the stairs.

His worst fright occurred one night when he saw the latch of his bedroom door lift. A white-haired old lady wearing a black cape passed through the room and vanished through the wardrobe. Mr Wood was terrified and slept with the light on after this event.

He made enquiries of his friends and relations, and his cousin Mrs Brittlebank told him of her own experiences in the cottage while he was in hospital. She had been staying there to look after her 80 year old aunt, Mr Wood's mother, during the final weeks of her life. She recalled one night when she had seen strange flickering lights which seemed to appear in one corner of the room, then dart about the room, finally coming to hover over the sleeping Mrs Wood. On another occasion, she had seen the bedroom door latch lift, and two figures enter the room then disappear. Both these phenomena had occurred shortly before Mrs Wood's death.

He also discovered that the previous owner of the cottage had experienced ghostly happenings, including one evening when a rug his wife was pegging was torn violently from her lap and hurled into the corner of the room. Their pet cat had fled in terror seconds before the event took place.

Mr Wood called in the services of a medium, who told him that there was a supernatural presence in the building, which had some connection with an old man and a dog. She also thought that there could be a body buried under the cottage.

Events began to get more frequent and more disturbing. Lights were switched on and off, heavy footsteps were heard, and the sound of a growling dog coming from the fireplace. Pots and pans seemed to be thrown about, there were sudden drops in temperature, and curtains were ripped down. Mrs Brittlebank even had a cardigan torn from her shoulders.

The most terrifying event of all took place when Mr Wood was attempting to relay a flagstone in the floor. He had prised the flag up, and had begun to shovel soil from beneath it, when Mrs Brittlebank saw a horrific shape emerge from the ground, then leap away and disappear. It seemed to be a large dog.

Although the cottage was exorcised on more than one occasion, things were going from bad to worse. Mr Wood decided that he could live in his home no longer, and both he and his cousin moved out of the village to live in Leek.

LONGTON

Ghosts at Longton Hall

WHEN Roy Whitfield was 15 he liked to gather with his friends on a grassy bank, the site of a former pottery spoil heap, to have a laugh and a gossip. Their main occupations, as Roy remembers, were smoking Woodbines and talking about girls. The location they frequented was on the lane from Longton to Blurton, and about 200 yards from where Longton Hall once stood.

One summer evening in 1943 he was there with three of his pals when they heard hysterical shouting. Roy thought he recognised the voice of a young man of his acquaintance. The four of them got up to investigate, and saw the youth approaching them, running as if his life depended on it and still shouting wildly.

He seemed extremely relieved to see Roy and his friends. When he'd managed to partially overcome his agitation, he blurted out that he'd seen a ghost. It was a girl in white, drifting along by the site of Longton Hall. His

consternation had turned to hysteria when the ghostly figure had passed right through him. 'There was no way he
was faking,' Roy recalls. 'He was really terrified.'

Over the years that followed, Roy heard of many others
who had seen the girl in white. His investigations in the
local library led him to believe that she was the ghost of a
girl who worked at Longton Hall in the 18th century.
Although the young lady worked at the hall, she lived
out, in a nearby farmhouse. She was horrified when she
found that she had been made pregnant by someone at
the hall, and had taken her life by drowning herself in a
pool in the grounds.

Although Longton Hall was demolished in 1934, the
farmhouse is still there, and so is the poor girl in white.
Many years after Roy Whitfield first heard about her, he
was enjoying a quiet drink in his local. Suddenly a white-
faced motorist came in. He informed the landlord that he'd
just driven through a ghost. It was the same girl in white.
She had appeared suddenly in front of his car, and he
feared he'd run over her, but when he stopped to look, she
had disappeared. He hadn't run over her, he had run
through her!

The driver was quite relieved when Roy told him that he
was just one of many people who had seen the ghost of the
girl in white from Longton Hall.

Sixty years ago, Mrs Gretta Earnest used to work as an
enameller at Chapman's pot bank in Longton. She used to
walk to work with her friend Hilda Bould who lived at
Longton Hall, and spent many happy weekends and holi-
days staying there. On several occasions she saw the ghost
of a lady dressed in a cloak and a feathered hat. Gretta
recalls one occasion when they came in very late, at about
midnight. The lady in the feathered hat glided past them,
without looking at them.

Gretta asked about the figure, and was told that it was
the ghost of the wife of a previous owner of the hall who
was murdered by her husband when he discovered her
fondness for one of the grooms. After shooting the groom,
he battered his wife to death in a violent jealous rage,

throwing her repeatedly against a wall. This ghost is often reputed to appear every New Year's Eve, on the anniversary of her death, though Mrs Earnest saw her on other occasions too.

Gretta tells me that her husband's grandfather was a painter and decorator, and was employed to paint the room where the murder took place. He frequently told his family that he was unable to remove the dark brown bloodstain from the wall. Gretta believes that the ghost she saw was on her way back to the room where the crime took place.

MAYFIELD

The Cottage in Gallowstree Lane

SO many weird and strange things have occurred to artist Jacqueline Burton-Naylor during the 35 years she has lived in her present home that she finds it hard to know where to begin. Although the deeds to her cottage in Gallowstree Lane only go back to the 1800s, the building is over 400 years old. With the neighbouring cottage, it was once an inn called The Mason's Arms.

Jacqueline's home is three storeys high, apart from a single storey section comprising the kitchen, bathroom and utility room. This extension was built with stones from Calwich Abbey, carried from there on a handcart. The abbey is one and a half miles away on the road to Ellastone, and was a monastery until the 1530s when it became a private house. Although it is over 460 years since monks lived at Calwich Abbey, one seems to have come to Jacqueline Burton-Naylor's cottage along with the stones.

Jacqueline's mother Margaret saw the monk one evening in 1985. He was at the top of the stairs that lead to the large studio-bedroom at the top of the house. The lower landing light was on, and there was still enough daylight to illuminate the stairs. She saw the monk quite clearly; he was dressed in a brown habit, a gold tasselled cord around his waist, and 'Jesus' sandals on his feet. His cowl was over his head, so that she couldn't see his face properly. She experienced no feeling of fear, and she was able to observe him for some ten to twelve seconds before he disappeared.

Some months later, Margaret was in the same upper floor bedroom, closing the curtains, when she felt someone tap her three times on her right shoulder. Assuming it was Jacqueline, she turned to find there was no one there.

The room is now Jacqueline's, and over the years she has heard voices, and ornaments being moved around in the dark. Electric lights come on by themselves, and the family cats frequently 'see' things, one of them, Alice, being driven quite wild at times. One of the most disturbing of these strange happenings is the three loud knocks sometimes heard coming from Jacqueline's wooden bedhead, since this always seems to precede a death in the family. One night in 1993 she was just dropping off to sleep when she heard an almighty thump hit her bedside cabinet. She put on the light and there in the middle of the floor was a lump of 'raw' limestone about the size of a tennis ball. She had never seen it before, and has no idea where it came from. It became a conversation-piece ornament on her shelf for a while, but has since disappeared. 'If it returns, I do hope it doesn't hit anyone!' Jacqueline says.

In 1966 she was alone in the house and was in the lounge, lying on the settee with her back to the front door. Her labrador Jason was on the carpet next to her, when both Jacqueline and the dog heard the gate open and close. Footsteps came up the front yard, and Jason got up and growled, the hair on his back bristling. Seeing a shadow through the window, Jacqueline went to open the door. A knock came just as she got there, but although she opened it immediately, there was no one there. 'It was not my imagination,' Jacqueline insists, 'and in any case the dog heard it too.' She has since had a glass panel put in the door so that she can see anyone approaching.

Jacqueline doesn't know whether the strange events that occur are connected in some way with the stone from Calwich Abbey, or possibly with the graveyard that forms the boundary of her home.

Jacqueline's father, Jack Burton, who died in 1983, was a heavy cigarette smoker. He is buried in the cemetery behind the cottage. Although no one now smokes in the house, the family have often walked into a wall of cigarette smoke while crossing the room. If they are sitting down, the smoke wafts over them.

Although Jacqueline's ex-husband was very sceptical, and he neither heard nor saw any mysterious phenomena when he lived in the cottage, the female members of the family do seem to have psychic abilities. Margaret 'knows' news items before they have appeared on the television or radio. Jacqueline too is aware what is about to happen before it actually occurs, though she is very keen to dismiss the notion that she is in any way weird. 'I would like to develop my ESP further,' she says.

It seems that Jacqueline's young daughter Sasha-Jayne has inherited the abilities of her mother and grandmother. She frequently knows when her father is going to visit, and reads what Jacqueline is thinking with ease. On one occasion, when shown a photograph of her late grandfather, she said that she had seen him. Asked if she meant that she had seen pictures of him, Sasha-Jayne replied, 'No, I've seen him around the house'.

MILFORD

The Ghost on a Bike

IN June 1949 Wilf and Violet Daniels set out early to drive down to visit Wilf's sister in Sussex. They left Stafford at six o'clock and had just passed through Milford when they topped a rise. Ahead of them they saw a cyclist, a solidly built man wearing a dark serge jacket and trousers, and riding an old fashioned sit-up-and-beg bike.

Wilf pulled out to overtake him, leaving him plenty of room. As the bonnet of Wilf's Standard 9 drew level with the bike's back wheel, the man and his cycle both disappeared. Wilf was absolutely astonished. 'I had seen the impossible,' he recalled. 'In broad daylight, a solid figure pedalling a solid bicycle had vanished before my eyes. The hair on the nape of my neck bristled and my spine had crushed ice slithering down it!'

He managed to stammer an awkward question to Violet, sitting beside him with two year old Michael on her lap, asking her whether she had seen anything. Pale faced and trembling, she confessed that she too had seen the cyclist until he simply disappeared.

When the Daniels family reached their destination, Wilf told his sister Dorothy about their experience. She was not surprised and informed him that the stretch of road between Milford and Rugeley had always been reputedly haunted. She thought it was something to do with a fatal accident in the area.

Some weeks later when Wilf was back at work, he was again recounting the incident. One of his colleagues, who lived at Great Haywood, about two miles from the stretch of road under discussion, was able to give Wilf more information. The accident that Dorothy referred to had occurred when a water engineer fell to his death down a deep shaft at a pumping station. This was situated in a walled garden opposite the lane to Weetman's Bridge.

The man had choked to death at the bottom of the vertical bore shaft, and his body had been brought up by a fireman named Coglan who volunteered to be lowered down in a bucket. The dead engineer had always cycled to work along the stretch of road where Wilf and Vi had seen their vanishing ghost-on-a-bike, and the spot had been the location of many strange sightings ever since his terrible, fatal accident.

RUGELEY

The Ghost at Brindley's Bank

THE ghost seen by two Rugeley women in 1939 was a blood-curdling sight. It was a summer evening and they were by the canal at the spot known as the Bloody Steps, close to Brindley's Bank. Hearing a wailing cry, they looked up and there he was. His feet were hidden in a foggy vapour but the rest of him was plainly visible. He had long black hair, and a doleful expression on his face. His clothes were black and white, and he was wearing knickerbockers. As they watched, he glided across the grass in front of them and disappeared through the railings of the waterworks.

The name of the Bloody Steps dates back to 1839, and the tragic murder of Christina Collins. She was a young married woman travelling from Liverpool to London to be with her husband Robert, who had obtained employment there. Her mode of travel was by barge on the Trent and Mersey Canal, but she was first molested and then brutally murdered by the drunken crew, two of whom were hanged for the crime, and a third sentenced to transportation. The three men, James Owen, George Thomas and William Ellis, threw Christina's body into the canal, where it was discovered on 17th June 1839. The steps up which her body was carried became known as the Bloody Steps, as it was claimed that they were stained by the blood dripping from her body.

Christina Collins' body was buried in Rugeley churchyard, and the tragic facts are recorded on her tombstone. It was to this grave that the two women made their way in 1939, following their terrifying experience by the canal. Their feeling of awe and ill-ease was not lessened when they discovered that their sighting of the ghost at Brindley's Bank had occurred on the 100th anniversary of Christina Collins' murder.

But who was the ghost? After some research and a great

deal of deliberation, they thought that it was likely to be that of Robert Collins, Christina's husband. The young newly-weds were known to have been deeply in love, and Christina was overheard by witnesses to cry out for him just before she was murdered. It may be that the desolate ghost of Robert Collins still haunts the scene of his wife's untimely death.

John Godwin, a local writer, has written a great deal about the murder. A few years ago, he was approached by thriller writer Colin Dexter who asked John if he would have any objections to him borrowing and adapting the story to form the plot of an Inspector Morse novel. John had no problem with this, and the novel was published as *The Wench Is Dead*. The story is basically the same, but the location transferred to Oxford. The book was made into a full-length television film in 1994, with John Thaw again playing the role of Inspector Morse.

The Death of John Landor

ELIZA HODGKINSON was a young nurse, and one Sunday in March 1782 she was asked if she would go immediately to Rugeley Grammar School to look after seven year old John Landor, who was gravely ill. John, the son of the rector of Colton, had been visited by his mother and her sister. They were distressed by his condition and Mrs Landor had sent for Eliza, asking her to sit up through the night with him.

The Landors sent their groom William Corser to walk the short distance to the school with Eliza. They set out at 8.30 pm, William carrying a lantern to light the way. As they approached the canal bridge, which was by Rugeley church, a woman in a brown cloak came up to them. She seemed to know who they were, because she asked them whether the rector was at home in Colton.

'Yes, he is,' Eliza replied, 'but he will not welcome any visitors this evening. He has enough on his mind.'

'But I must see him,' the woman said. 'I have a child that needs to be buried tonight.'

Startled, Eliza and William glanced down and saw that the woman was carrying a bundle under her cloak. The shape was like that of a small coffin, but before they could say anything further, the woman disappeared. William held his lantern high and the two of them searched along the path, but there was no sign of her, so the bewildered couple continued to walk to the school. Eliza kept watch over the sick child that night, returning to Colton the next day. The rector had seen nothing at all of the strange woman with the dead child. The next night, Eliza Hodgkinson nursed John Landor again, but he died while she was there. In her heart, she wondered whether the encounter the previous night was meant to warn her that the child would die.

Eliza did not tell anyone about her meeting with the woman by the canal bridge, but William Corser did. Although in the years that followed, many people tried to question her about the incident, she still refused to give any details. However, in 1838, when she was an old lady, she made a sworn statement to a solicitor, giving the whole story.

SHOBNALL

Legends of Sinai House

THE haunted Sinai House is a moated, half-timbered building which has stood on high ground at Shobnall, near Burton-on-Trent, for many centuries. Its two wings were built in the early 1400s and the central portion in the 17th century, though the moat dates back to 1334. It was originally the Great Lodge of the manor of Schobenhale (Shobnall), and by 1410 it was held by Burton Abbey. Monks from the abbey were allowed to go to Sinai three times a year, to enjoy the delights of Sinai Park, and to meet relatives. It was also used as a sanatorium when they were ill or recovering from blood-letting.

In the reign of Henry VIII, it was taken from the abbey and given into the possession of Sir William Paget who used it as a residence for his steward William Wyatt.

On a postcard printed at the beginning of this century it is shown as a stuccoed farmhouse. Today all of the stucco has gone, together with the windows and most of the roof, leaving a sadly dilapidated building. Some of the neglect dates back to World War II when members of the RAF were billeted there. Even in its present condition it retains all of its powerful atmosphere and much of its 'presence'. All is not lost. Visiting Sinai House on a wet Sunday afternoon in March 1994, I met its new owner, Kate Newton, who intends first to make one wing habitable, then to work on the rest of the house ' ... even if it takes the rest of my life!'

One of the most persistent legends of Sinai tells of a secret underground passage from the house to Burton Abbey. The fact that there seems no rational reason for creating such a tunnel, plus the physical impossibility of building it, count for little in the locality, and the story is still widely believed. The discovery of a blocked entrance in the cellars of the house has only served to renew the legend.

Sinai House and the surrounding fields were the childhood playground of Nigel Slater who accompanied me on my visit. He was keen that I should see the 'Grey Lady' tree, which stood about half a mile from the building. This was a very old, limbless hollow tree, 20 ft tall and shaped like a hooded man carrying something in his arms. The legend he told me, gleaned from the old folk of the area, was of a monk who obviously interpreted 'the enjoyment of the delights of Sinai Park' in the wrong way. This wayward monk met a young peasant girl, and their friendship led to her becoming pregnant. The legend alleges that he murdered her to prevent the discovery of his deed, then carried her half a mile from the sanatorium and buried her under the tree. The tree died, and over the years it metamorphosed until its shape revealed the monk carrying the dead girl.

Nigel last visited the tree to photograph it in June 1993, but he was insistent that when I saw the real thing it would convey more than its photograph. He was devastated to find that somewhere between June 1993 and March 1994 it had been uprooted and removed, leaving only a circular depression in the ground. He feels that not only has part of his childhood gone, but also a vital element of the local heritage has been taken.

What may still remain is the Grey Lady, the ghost seen on the bridge over the moat at Sinai House, usually on New Year's Eve. She has been seen there on many occasions, though if, as Nigel Slater believes, she is the murdered girl who walks from the house to the site of her burial, then she predates the bridge which bears the date 1732.

It may be that Sinai House has more than one ghost. If so, the lady seen on the 18th century bridge may be from a later period than the ghost of the murdered girl.

Sinai House is not, as I originally assumed from its religious history, named after the biblical Mount Sinai. On older documents it is written Seyne House, and is said to be a corruption of an old French word meaning 'a holiday and its associated privileges'. A good view of Sinai House can be had from the public footpath which borders the property, but casual visitors should bear in mind that the house itself is private. Apart from anything else, trespassers would be risking life and limb if they should enter the building in its present condition!

SILVERDALE

A Visit from a Soldier Son

MRS AGNES RAE and Mrs Ethel Gorton are twin sisters, and although they live 300 miles apart, they are able to share many strange and beautiful experiences. Each knows what is happening to the other, and they even share the same dreams. They come of a family which all had the ability to see things before they happen. Agnes and Ethel were brought up by their grandmother in the village of Silverdale, their mother being dead. Both of them, Agnes from Falkirk and Ethel from Fenton, have told me about a psychic event that happened to their grandmother during the 1914-18 war.

She had a 22 year old son, Agnes' and Ethel's Uncle Jim, who was serving in the army in France. One summer afternoon, grandmother was busy peeling potatoes in the kitchen, when she was suddenly aware that someone was standing behind her. She heard a voice say, 'Mother,' and she turned to see her soldier son. He gave her a lovely smile, but told her not to try to touch him. She sat down and Jim said that he had passed over but that there was something in the post for her. After saying, 'Forget me not,' he smiled at her again and disappeared as suddenly as he had come.

She knew that something terrible had happened to her son, and was not surprised therefore when the postman knocked on the door later that day. He had the telegram in his hand that all wives and mothers dreaded; it told her that Jim had been gassed in the trenches in France. The next day the postman was back with a small parcel for her. It was from Jim. When she opened it, there was a golden heart on a chain. On it was engraved 'Mother – Forget Me Not'. Ethel recalls that her grandmother wore that heart every Poppy Day.

Ethel says that although Jim died before she and Agnes were born, they often saw and heard him in that house. There was an organ that belonged to him, and the girls used to hear it playing if ever either of them were alone in the house. One night, Ethel recalls that both of them saw two men in miners' clothing climbing up the stairs while they were lying in bed. As both Jim and his brother David were miners at Silverdale pit before the war, the girls were sure they had seen the ghost of Uncle Jim again. 'They never believed us,' Ethel says, 'but it's all true.'

STAFFORD

The Ghost in a Police Hostel

IN 1968 Ron Fields was a police cadet with the Staffordshire police force. He was based in a cadet hostel in the grounds of Baswich House in Stafford. The hostel was an old building formerly used as servants' quarters.

One weekend in November, the cadets had been on an Outward Bound course in the Peak District. On the Sunday night, most of the other cadets returned to their parents' homes but since Ron was due to start work early on the Monday morning, he decided to sleep in the hostel.

When he got back to Baswich, he found that the hostel was locked up and empty. However Ron was a resourceful police cadet, and he soon had the window open and gained access to the building.

As he lay in bed, he was astonished to hear the sound of footsteps coming from the upstairs landing. He knew that there was no one else in the building. He recalls that the footsteps were steady and unhurried. He tried to put the sounds out of his mind, and was relieved when they stopped some 20 minutes later. But then he experienced the inexplicable sensation that someone had entered his room, although the light from the window was sufficient to show him there was no one there. Then to Ron's horror, he felt the weight of the unknown person sit on the bed. After enduring this for a minute or two, Ron sat up and the weight disappeared from his bed.

The following day, the other cadets returned to the hostel and Ron confided his strange experience to his room-mate Dave Smith. In Ron's words, his friend 'fell about laughing'. However, two weeks later, Dave spent a Sunday night alone in the hostel and changed his tune. 'You know that story you told me,' he said to Ron, 'well, I certainly believe you now. Last night the exact same thing happened to me. I heard the footsteps upstairs and felt someone come in and sit on my bed.'

The two cadets made a vow to keep the story to themselves, as they guessed that they would be the butt of jokes from their colleagues if they spoke openly about the hostel ghost.

They did try to track down the history of the building and heard that a servant had once hanged himself there after falling in love with one of the maids. Although the girl had returned his feelings, their employer had disapproved of their romance and had forbidden them to see each other. On hearing about this tragedy, Ron and Dave thought it probable that the ghostly footsteps might be those of the hanged servant, returning to the bedside of his forbidden lady-love.

Dave is no longer a policeman, but Ron Fields is now a police sergeant. As he still fears the mockery of his colleagues, I have changed his name.

The Haunted House in Newport Street

IN 1963 Frederick Gee, a director of a local building company, was asked by a long-standing customer to do a survey of an old house in which an elderly aunt had just died. Frederick collected the keys and went to the house in Newport Street, Stafford, to check whether any repairs were necessary before the house was put on the market. Upstairs Frederick was immediately fascinated by a magnificent long-case clock. As he had an interest in clocks, he went over to it and set it to strike twelve.

As it did so, he heard a voice downstairs cry out, 'Are you there?' He called back, 'I'll be down in a minute'. When the clock had finished striking, Frederick went downstairs but there was no one there. He wasn't too concerned about the incident, though he did think that the way the clock striking twelve conjured up the voice was a little eerie.

Eventually, Frederick Gee sent the customer an estimate

for replastering some damp patches, which he estimated would take a plasterer and mate about three or four days' work. The customer accepted the estimate and Frederick took the men and materials to the house. On the second day he returned and was surprised to find that they had virtually completed the work. When he congratulated them on their speed, they informed him that they wanted to get away from the house as quickly as possible. They had been driven mad by someone in the house whistling. 'We've searched everywhere,' they said, 'but we can't find where the bugger is. We reckon the bloody house is haunted.' Wisely, Frederick refrained from telling them about his own experience.

STOKE-ON-TRENT

Mary, Mary, Quite Contrary

JENNY ALLSOP lives in a modernised terraced house in Sheppards Street, in the West End area of Stoke-on-Trent. As soon as she moved in, in November 1989, she thought there was something strange about her kitchen. She frequently felt that there was someone standing behind her, and there was often a very cold spot in the room. Once when Jenny got up in the night to visit her downstairs bathroom, she noticed a shadow in the kitchen doorway and felt a rush of air pass her.

She had been told by neighbours that an old lady died in the front room of the house, and Jenny has named her ethereal visitor 'Mary'. One or two things continue to be a puzzle. Why does Mary seem to haunt the kitchen when she died in the front room? And why do Jenny's cats and dog seem oblivious of Mary's ghostly presence? 'I always thought that animals were more sensitive to ghosts,' Jenny told me, 'but mine seem to take no notice of Mary at all.'

Perhaps the kitchen was Mary's favourite spot in the house and the ghost likes to visit it. And if she loved animals when she was alive, could it be that she is careful not to disturb them? Or is Mary simply being as contrary as her nursery rhyme namesake?

STONE

Entombed

THE ghost that haunted the churchyard of the town of Stone in the 1780s led to a most macabre discovery. The apparition of a young man was first seen in the autumn of 1781, and was soon identified as being Tom Meaykin. Tom had been buried in the churchyard of St Michael's in July of that year, following his sudden death at the age of 21.

Thomas Meaykin had been born in the moorlands village of Rushton Spencer but had left the village to seek work in Stone. There he had become a houseboy to the local apothecary, with responsibility for looking after the horses. He was happy in his work and a popular local figure. His only problem, if indeed it was a problem, was that his employer's pretty young daughter had fallen in love with him. Tom was very conscious of the difference in their stations, but the young lady had set her cap at Tom in a very determined and public fashion.

The whole population of Stone was amused by the situation, but when the apothecary finally realised what was happening, he was furious at the way his social reputation was being undermined. He remonstrated with his headstrong daughter, but she refused to budge. She wanted Tom and she would have him. Then suddenly Tom died and was buried in St Michael's churchyard.

After the frequent appearances of his ghost throughout the autumn and winter of 1781-2, tongues began to wag. Wasn't it rather convenient for the apothecary that the problem of his daughter's infatuation for the houseboy had been solved so easily? And wouldn't someone in his profession have all manner of deadly poisons to hand?

About a year after Tom's death it was decided to re-open his grave and exhume the body. A terrible sight met the eyes of those present: Tom's body was now lying face down, whereas it had been buried in the normal position. The implications were obvious. When Tom had been buried, he had not been dead! He had been deeply unconscious, but alive. As the people of Stone contemplated the dreadful image of the young man coming round in his coffin, buried six ft beneath the earth, they were horrified. It was no wonder that Tom's ghost had returned to haunt the scene of his living death. It was widely believed that his employer had drugged the boy into a coma before having him buried, though it could never be proved.

His body was reinterred in the churchyard of St Lawrence's, in his native village of Rushton Spencer in July 1782. The worn inscription on his gravestone can still be deciphered. In a mixture of Latin, English and Greek it tells of his 'death by violence, caused by the wickedness of man'. This time, Tom's body was buried the wrong way round, with his head to the east and feet to the west. This was done in order to lay his ghost.

SWINSCOE

Diana Dors and the Scottish Soldier

IN 1962 the beautiful film star Diana Dors was staying in a 16th century cottage in a tiny Staffordshire village. She was appearing in a show in Ashbourne, in aid of St Monica's Church of England Children's Home. Ashbourne is in Derbyshire, but after each performance Miss Dors would drive five miles west, across the river Dove into Staffordshire, to the village of Swinscoe.

On the Thursday night of her stay, she awoke to see the figure of a man with long flowing hair in her room! She was both alarmed and annoyed, but he was neither a devoted fan nor a besotted admirer. Miss Dors quickly realised that the haggard figure was not that of a living being but an apparition. She later stated to a local newspaper, 'It certainly had long hair and was pretty horrible. I was scared'.

She investigated further and heard that other people who'd stayed there had also seen the ghost. She came to believe it was the ghost of a Jacobite soldier, killed between Ashbourne and Swinscoe in 1745.

In that year, the Scottish soldiers of Bonnie Prince Charlie advanced as far south as Derby, before deciding to retreat. The men were very dispirited by the time they reached Ashbourne, and it is known that a number of them were caught there by George II's troops. There is a strong local tradition that Hanging Bridge over the river Dove took its name from the large number of hangings of Scottish soldiers, although historians can find no evidence of this. It is certain though that many Highland soldiers met their deaths in the area, as they began their long retreat north.

Diana Dors firmly believed that the long-haired ghost she saw in 1962 was that of one of the Highlanders, still haunting the place of his death.

SWYTHAMLEY

The Ghost of Lud's Church

LUD'S church is not a building at all, but a deep rocky ravine, 50 ft deep and 200 ft long, hidden among the trees of Forest Wood on the steep slopes of the Dane valley. This secret chasm is said to have been a hiding place for both Robin Hood and Friar Tuck, but the ghost that haunts Lud's church is that of a young lady who met her death there in the early 15th century.

Her name was Alice and she was the granddaughter of Walter de Lud Auk, a keen supporter of the doctrines of John Wycliffe. These reformers, known as Lollards, used the natural cathedral of the secret chasm to hold their services, hidden away from the eyes of the Church establishment and the soldiers of Henry V.

However on the fatal day in question, Lud Auk was leading 14 of his followers, including Alice, in a service. The narrow cave at the entrance to the ravine was guarded by the head forester, Henrick Montair.

Unfortunately the hymn singing of the band of Lollards was so ardent and so loud that it was heard by passing soldiers. One of them rushed towards the ravine calling on the reformers to yield in the name of the king. Some of the Lollards reached for their swords but the 70 year old Lud Auk told them to show restraint. Most did, but Montair hurled the soldier back towards his own men. One soldier loosed an arrow at the forester but it sped past him and struck the 18 year old Alice. She collapsed and died in her grandfather's arms.

The broken-hearted Lollards sang a funeral hymn for her, so moving that even the soldiers were in tears. The body of the dead girl was buried in the entrance to the ravine before the Lollards surrendered to the king's men and were taken into captivity. The forester, Montair, managed to escape to France but Walter de Lud Auk died in prison, still mourning Alice's death.

Alice's ghost was seen in Lud's church many times in the centuries that followed, including more recent sightings in the 1930s, the 1950s, and once in 1977. In 1959 she was seen by Josie and Ann Holland, and in September 1977 by a hiker, Ben Peters.

For many years, the wooden figurehead from the ship *Swythamley* stood in Lud's church (Swythamley Hall is about a mile away). The white figurehead was of a young girl, and it was placed in the chasm as a tribute to Alice. However it was smashed by vandals a few years ago, and now the only figure that haunts Lud's church is less substantial than the wooden one, though it has lasted much longer. Alice's ghost still wanders the place of her death.

The Green Knight and the Wallabies

IN the 14th century saga *Sir Gawain and the Green Knight* Gawain is King Arthur's favourite cousin and the original hero of the first quest for the Holy Grail. He travels to the Green Chapel and there slays the giant Green Knight, the symbol of death and rebirth. Scholars have concluded that the Green Knight of Arthurian legend was probably based on the ubiquitous Green Man who occurs throughout English medieval folklore as a fertility figure. Thus Gawain's slaying and decapitating of this figure represents the annual 'death' and rebirth of trees, flowers and crops.

Lud's church has recently been claimed as the legendary Green Chapel, and it does fit the description of the spot described in the Arthurian saga. David Clarke, in his *Ghosts & Legends of the Peak District* associates the Green Knight with the Celtic sun-god Lugh and he thinks that Lud's church may well be a corruption of Lugh's church.

Stories of the ghosts at Lud's church include not only Alice Lud Auk; many hobs and boggarts have been seen, and even a headless green giant, lending credence to the Green Knight story. Could the creators of the saga of

Gawain slaying the Green Man have based it on the stories associated with this area of north Staffordshire? It seems quite possible.

And the wallabies? Visitors have seen these Australian marsupials in this area too, and have thought that they might be hallucinating or seeing ghosts. But these animals are neither supernatural creatures nor the result of too many pints of beer in the local inns. In 1938 Swythamley Hall, the home of the Brocklehurst family, boasted a private zoo. The last member of that family was killed in action during the Second World War, and thus never returned. A group of wallabies escaped from the zoo into the wild, and despite the bleak conditions and very cold winters they have bred in the area, developing shaggy coats which have helped them to survive for over 50 years! The police at the station in Leek are quite used to bewildered visitors calling to say, 'Honestly, I haven't been drinking, but I've been walking up in the Roaches and I swear I've just seen a little kangaroo!'

TAMWORTH

Ghostly Ladies in Black and White

IT is hardly surprising that Tamworth Castle has its fair share of ghosts. Tamworth was once the royal capital of the kingdom of Mercia, and its castle is over 1,000 years old.

One of the ghosts that haunts the castle is that of the White Lady, said to walk the battlements. The White Lady was the mistress of a knight named Sir Tarquin. A tournament was taking place in Lady's Meadow below the castle walls, and as she watched from the terrace, she saw her knight killed in combat by Sir Lancelot, the hero of Arthurian legend. She still weeps as she makes her nightly promenade, mourning the death of her lover.

Tamworth Castle also boasts a Black Lady, the ghost of one of the Benedictine nuns expelled from their abbey in nearby Polesworth by Baron Roger le Marmion. He did this on receiving the grant of Tamworth from William the Conqueror, soon after 1066. In 1139 the ghost of the Black Lady appeared to a later Lord Marmion, reputed to have been a wicked and licentious man. The nun's ghost warned him that he would die a horrible death unless the abbey and its lands were restored to the Benedictine order. Having spoken, she then struck him a blow on his side with her staff, creating a terrible wound. Over the months that followed, the injury could not be healed, and Lord Marmion reluctantly decided to carry out the wishes of his ghostly tormentor. He restored the Polesworth abbey to its former owners and the wound in his side healed. However his health may not have been fully restored, as he died four years later. It is often claimed that the Black Lady is in fact the ghost of St Editha.

Visitors to Tamworth Castle are able to visit the 'Ghost Room' where the Black Lady appears, and are also shown a murder room, the site of another haunting.

Barbara Adams has worked at the castle for 19 years, and has grown used to its ghostly residents. Her first encounter occurred when she was accompanying the senior attendant, and they entered what is now the shop. At that time it was a storeroom. Both of them felt a terrible pressure, as if they were being crushed. She describes it as a nasty experience.

A much later manifestation was seen more recently, when a security video system was being installed. The camera picked up a white shape in the Great Hall. It floated across the hall, then shot off in another direction. The whole event lasted for about twelve minutes and was picked up by the camera. Barbara and a colleague went to the Great Hall to investigate. They felt an unusual chill, but could see nothing. Later, an engineer checked the camera equipment and found that it was working correctly; he had no explanation for the white 'shadow'.

Barbara says that a number of visitors have felt the presence of the ghost, and like her, they report a sudden drop in temperature. Barbara talks to the ghost, telling it that she knows it's there but that it is not going to frighten her away.

One of her fellow attendants at the castle is David Nickels. He is certain that there is something supernatural there, and says that on one occasion as he ran up the staircase he felt something running with him.

Valerie Lee had a much more scary experience. She came up against the ghost one dark evening as she went to lock a door in the tower. She was on the stairs, when the outside door slammed to and locked itself from the outside. This door was fastened open with a large hook, and Valerie knows there was no one around who could have undone the hook, then slammed the door and locked her in. No living human, that is! She admits that she panicked a bit. Fortunately she was able to radio for someone to come and release her from her dark tower.

Ghostly Footsteps in St Editha's Church

> 'As I was going up the stair
> I met a man who wasn't there'

IF you climb the spiral stone stairs in the south-west turret of the tower of St Editha's church in Tamworth, you are likely – just like the man in Hughes Mearns' poem – to meet a man who isn't there! As you ascend the steps, you may hear the sounds of footsteps descending towards you. You may stop and wonder how the two of you will be able to pass safely. But though the footsteps are above you one minute and below you the next, you will see nothing.

This phenomenon has caused many a visitor to wonder if the footsteps are spectral rather than human. After all, how has the descending owner of the footsteps passed from above you to below you? A church ghost, surely.

There is a non-supernatural explanation. The arrangement of the staircases in St Editha's church tower is most unusual. There are two of them, one entered from the churchyard, the other from the interior of the church. They are designed so that the roof of one staircase forms the floor of the other. If you are climbing one staircase, you can hear the footsteps of anyone descending the other, though you will never meet!

This architectural oddity is extremely rare, though there is another example of it in the Château de Chambord in France. An illustration of the idea can also be seen in one of Leonardo da Vinci's cartoons. One further strange fact about the two sets of stairs in the Tamworth church is that one has 101 steps, and the other has 106.

TEAN

Martha, The Unquiet Woman

WHEN Mrs Freda Beardmore was a girl, she lived with her parents, two sisters and four brothers in an old house attached to a shop called The Bon Marche. Downstairs, the house had two living-rooms with wooden boards on the lower half of the walls. There were wooden seats, a fireplace and a small window leading through to the parlour. If this description sounds like the interior of a public house, this is because the house was indeed a pub called The Quiet Woman in former times. Freda adds, 'It wasn't very quiet when we were all inside, I can tell you!' There was also a big rambling kitchen where there used to be a well until Freda's dad, Jack Camwell, filled it in.

Jack was a miner at New Haden pit, and when he was on the night shift he would sleep in the third storey room during the daytime. Freda and her brothers and sisters liked to explore the attic rooms when their father wasn't sleeping there. It was up in these attic rooms that they saw and heard the resident ghost, known as Martha, the Quiet

Woman. Freda says that the children were so used to seeing the ghost that they were not too frightened of her, but Mrs Camwell never believed them when they told her about Martha.

Jack told his children that Martha had been accused of being a witch, and she had been beheaded on the spot where the house now stood. Martha was supposed to have caused a lot of trouble in the village and the surrounding area. Her punishment sounds to have been an unofficial one, since the official penalty for witches in England was always death by hanging. (Death by burning was used for witches in Scotland and on the continent, but in England being burned at the stake was reserved solely for heretics.) It would seem that the beheading of Martha must have been the action of a mob acting outside the law.

Freda recalls that Martha often opened doors around the house, particularly at night, but her favourite trick was to tilt the pictures that hung on the walls. When anyone put the pictures straight again, they would hear female laughter coming from the top of the house, followed by a shadow passing in front of them.

Jack Camwell told Freda that when the place had been a pub, Martha used to set the spittoon spinning in the middle of the floor. She enjoyed playing tricks on the men who were drinking in the pub, trying to set them arguing and fighting. She had been an outspoken woman in her lifetime, and claimed that she had as much right to drink in a pub as any man. I wonder if this liberated claim, years ahead of its time, could have been the cause of her death, rather than the practising of witchcraft!

Whatever mischief Martha may have intended the menfolk of the pub, Freda Beardmore states categorically that the ghost never did her family any harm.

THORNCLIFFE

Mermaid's Pool

THE Mermaid's Pool, officially known as Blackmere, is situated in moorland about two miles north-east of Thorncliffe in the area known as Morridge, and close to the 1,603 ft hill, Merryton Low. It has always been held that no animal would drink from the pool, no bird fly over it, although this was disputed by the 17th century naturalist Robert Plot, who described his visit to the pool in his *Natural History of Staffordshire* of 1686.

Blackmere's greatest claim to fame is the mermaid said to inhabit its depths. She is a lady to avoid. Unlike her sister who inhabits the Mermaid's Pool on Kinder Scout in Derbyshire, the mermaid of Blackmere is no bringer of good fortune. The Blackmere mermaid entices any passerby who sees her into the pool and takes him down to a certain death by drowning.

One tradition alleges that the mermaid was in fact a beautiful young woman who was drowned in the waters of Blackmere after being accused of witchcraft by a rejected suitor, Joseph Linnett. Later the body of her accuser was found floating in the pool with the scratches of sharp talons on his face.

If you should seek refuge from this gruesome tale in the nearby inn, you will find no safe haven, for the inn is named The Mermaid, and on the wall it is written that if the mermaid 'calls on you to greet her, she ups and drags you down'.

At the end of the 19th century, workmen attempted to drain the pool, but they reported that the mermaid appeared and warned them that if the waters of Blackmere escaped the confines of the pool, the whole town of Leek would be drowned. Leek is still there, three miles away, and the pool is still there, so it seems that the workmen took the lady's threat seriously.

96

TIXALL

How Did I Get Here?

STRANDED in Rugeley one summer evening in 1990, Tony
Mercury decided to walk to Stafford, taking the route
through Little and Great Haywood. He had been hoping
that he might manage to hitch a lift, but at 12.30 am he was
still walking. Logically he should have been in the village
of Tixall, on the road that passes the church, but at this
point he became utterly confused. The road under his feet
simply disappeared and he suddenly found himself
amongst the gravestones of Tixall church but surrounded
by the trees of a dense wood.

Tony knew the area reasonably well, and he was aware
that there is no wood in that locality. He was understand-
ably frightened, and admits that he ran for dear life. Then,
just as suddenly, he found himself back on the road to
Stafford and continued his journey in a state of some puz-
zlement and shock.

Tony has been back to Tixall with his girlfriend Jacky,
but they have been unable to find anywhere that resembles
the wood he discovered in the middle of the night in 1990.
Wherever it was that he found himself that summer night,
Tony and Jacky are convinced that it isn't a location that
still exists in the late 20th century. Talking to a lady who
used to live in Tixall, Jacky discovered that other people
have had similar experiences, seeming to go back in time to
the Tixall of an earlier era.

TOMPKIN

The Skin of a Drummer Boy

THE small hamlet of Tompkin, about two miles south-east of Endon, owes its name to a macabre legend. When the supporters of Bonnie Prince Charlie came south in their vain attempt to restore a Stuart king to the English throne, they passed through Staffordshire. The Highland soldiers were forced to live off the land, and one party billeted themselves at the home of Squire Murhall. He thoroughly resented their presence but was unable or unwilling to stand up to his armed visitors. He no doubt ground his teeth in frustration while they slept in his house and ate his food, until they finally set off for the town of Leek.

Once they had left, Squire Murhall regained his courage and followed with a small number of his servants. He managed to capture one straggler, a wounded drummer-boy named Tam. He extracted his revenge for the humiliation he had suffered at the hands of the Scottish soldiers in the most brutal way. Tam was just 15, but the Squire had him flayed alive with the intention of having the boy's skin made into a drum.

Here the legends vary. One version says that the boy's skin was indeed made into a drum that was hung in St Luke's church in Endon. However, terrible calamities ensued, including crop failures and sudden deaths of livestock, and the drum was eventually taken from the church and buried.

The alternative version states that no one was able to tan the human skin, so the drum was never completed. Both legends agree that the ghost of the young Scottish drummer-boy has been seen in the Leek and Endon area ever since his terrible death in 1745. The spot where the boy's skin was buried was known as Tam's Skin, later corrupted to Tomkin and eventually Tompkin.

Squire Murhall did not escape completely. When Tam's comrades learned of his fate, they returned and beat the cruel squire within an inch of his life, leaving him permanently crippled. A vicious punishment, of course, though it is very hard not to feel that summary justice was done.

TUTBURY

Robin Hood and Clorinda, Queen of the Feast

NOW what is Robin Hood, claimed by both Nottinghamshire and the Barnsdale area of Yorkshire, doing in a book about Staffordshire? Well, Staffordshire has a claim too! One tradition puts the birthplace of the legendary outlaw hero at Loxley, near Bagot's Park, and it is said that Robin often returned to the Forest of Needwood when Sherwood grew too hot for him.

It was on one of these visits that he met the fair Clorinda, whose titles include the Queen of the Shepherds and the Queen of the Feast. Not only was Clorinda a beautiful young woman, she was also an excellent shot with the longbow.According to a 15th century ballad, Robin met Clorinda at Tutbury Fair. The dark-haired beauty was dressed in a gown of green velvet, and her skin was as smooth as glass. How could Robin resist a woman dressed in his favourite colour? He was immediately taken by her appearance and he invited Clorinda to dine with him.

She accepted his invitation and together they set out to find some fresh venison on the hoof. Robin's intention was to impress her by using his bow to shoot their dinner, but when they came across a herd of deer, it was Clorinda's arrow that did the trick. He was amazed and delighted, and at their al fresco picnic he declared his love for her. Obviously, Cupid was another successful archer that day.

After the meal, a parson was sent for and Robin and Clorinda went through a wedding ceremony, before consummating their love-at-first-sight affair.

I wonder what Maid Marian, presumably safely tucked away in Sherwood, made of all this? Did she ever hear about Robin's dalliance with the beautiful Clorinda? Was the great hero Robin Hood a philandering Lothario, or even a bigamist? Perhaps we should be charitable and just say that the ballad about Clorinda, Tutbury's Queen of the Feast, comes from a different tradition to the more widely known stories about Maid Marian.

A White Lady and a Norman Knight

IT is hardly surprising that Tutbury Castle has a number of ghosts. The castle must have been an old building when Robin Hood was a lad. There was certainly a fort there in Saxon times, and there may have been an Iron Age settlement before that. After the Norman Conquest, the castle was given to Henry de Ferrers, one of William the Conqueror's comrades-in-arms at the battle of Hastings.

The present resident custodian of the castle is Barry Vallens, who has been there since 1977. The first ghost he encountered was a monk-like figure in a brown robe. When Barry took over, the deep ditch that served as a moat was overgrown and full of rubbish. He was clearing it out one evening when he looked up to see a robed figure standing on top of the bank. Barry climbed up to see who it was but the figure had disappeared. A few weeks later, Barry saw him again on a different part of the ditch. This time Barry was higher up and could see the monk's face, but again the figure disappeared. These sightings took place in the part of the castle known as the Vinecroft, where hops were grown for making ale, for Tutbury was making beers long before the neighbouring town of Burton.

Barry, a no-nonsense man of Derbyshire farming stock, tells me that there was no way the figure could have left the Vinecroft without passing him. 'The figure simply vanished,' he says. The one thing that still puzzles Barry is why the monk's robe was brown, since the Cistercian monks who once lived in the nearby priory would have worn black.

Another ghost inhabits the watch tower, this time a lady in white. Barry dismisses the widely quoted tale that this is the ghost of Mary Queen of Scots, who was a prisoner at Tutbury Castle in 1569-70 and again in 1585-6. Barry is certain that the white lady is, in fact, 'Lady M' who met her death there in very peculiar circumstances. She was using the watch tower as a secret rendezvous, but when she arrived one night she found her lover dead, lying in a pool of blood. Hearing a sound behind her she turned, expecting to see her husband. However, it was the castle steward who stood there, with sword drawn. The steward later claimed that Lady M rushed at him and impaled herself on his sword, but when he told his tale he was himself slain by his master. Perhaps Lord M knew that 'dead men tell no tales' and preferred his wife's killer to remain permanently silent.

One afternoon in 1992 a party of school children from Stoke-on-Trent were visiting the castle. They had picnicked on the grass, when Barry noticed one young girl was crying. 'What's wrong?' he asked the teacher. 'Has she hurt herself?'

'No,' said the teacher, 'she's just being silly. She says she's seen a white lady in the tower.' The girl went on to tell Barry how she had run away when the white lady in the tower had stared at her. Barry questioned her further. She had never been to Tutbury before and neither had her parents; she had no knowledge of the White Lady legends. This ghost has been seen by many visitors to Tutbury Castle, though Barry himself has never seen her.

Talking in his sitting-room, once a bedroom slept in by Charles I, Barry described how he had often seen a grey shadow cross the doorway that leads to a second sitting-room. His daughter Lynne interrupted to say that she was present when her sister-in-law Jill had seen a grey lady crossing the same doorway. This was information that Barry didn't know, but which he added to his store of mysterious happenings at the castle.

'Then there is the Norman knight,' he told me. 'He's a frightful fellow.' The knight, who may be one of the Ferrers family, is buried in the chapel whose ruins are in the centre of the castle. The chapel was called the chapel of St Michael on the Hill in Saxon times, but was altered to St Peter's by the Normans. The ghost of the knight wishes to drive people from the castle, it seems. Once Barry picked up a silver and ivory glove ring from the chapel foundations and took it into his home to clean and examine it. He and his wife Betty then suffered a series of frights, including a disembodied hand that tapped on their window. The same week, Mr and Mrs Vallens were in bed when they heard a horrendous crashing from outside. Pausing to pick up his torch and shotgun, Barry rushed outside but could find nothing. 'No broken window,' he told me, 'and when I checked by daylight next day, no masonry damage of any kind.' Barry took the hint; he returned the ring to the chapel and the knight has not troubled him since.

Barry recalls that during his first six months as custodian, the castle seemed to be testing him. 'This place takes you over,' he states. 'You have to work with it, or everything goes wrong.' He then added ominously, 'But I have to make sure it doesn't dominate me!' He remembers with sadness Bella, his boxer bitch, who was afraid to go upstairs to the banqueting room. Despite being a strong swimmer, she was found drowned in the river on the first Boxing Day they spent at Tutbury. Lynne recalled that her cat would never go into the banqueting room, even when being carried.

One of Lynne' scariest moments occurred when she and her husband were sleeping in an upstairs room. Suddenly, they were woken by a tremendous banging. Lynne put on the light, to see that the open lid of their stereo was banging itself against the wall, although the vase of tall grasses next to it was perfectly still! Her terrified husband reached out and knocked the lid shut, and they hid under the covers. Another scare she recalls is when a large picture of Charles I fell from the wall, smashing the glass. When Lynne examined it, its cord was still intact and the picture hook still firmly attached to the wall.

Three girls from a catering college were employed by Barry to serve meals to visitors in the upstairs banqueting room. However, after one weekend, they were so disturbed by footsteps in the empty room that they left, deciding to have no more to do with Tutbury Castle.

Footsteps are frequently heard by members of the Vallens family, but they are not the first to hear them. When Barry spoke to Henry Ludlam who was custodian of the castle from 1909 to 1950, he found that most of the phenomena had also been experienced by his family.

UTTOXETER

A Lady with a Shock of Grey Hair

IN 1977 Geoff Startin was in his twenties. He remembers sitting in Uttoxeter Parish Church talking with his friend Alan. He looked up and saw the figure of a grey-haired old lady on the balcony. He was very puzzled at this, as he and Alan had just explored the whole building, and knew it to be empty. Moreover they were sitting by the door and no one had come in while they were there.

As he watched, the figure disappeared. Just as he began to wonder whether he had been taken in by a trick of the light, Alan asked him, 'Did you see her too?' He went on to describe the figure just as Geoff had seen her!

The two young men went up to the balcony to see if they could see the lady, but there was no one there. Geoff, now an Anglican clergyman in South Wales, can still remember the ghostly figure's shock of grey hair.

Geoff also remembers an incident that occurred in Uttoxeter in the late 1970s, when workmen at Bamford's factory in Pinfold Street were terrified by the ghost of a dark-haired woman in black. It was alleged to be the ghost of Emily Bamford who died in the 1880s. Emily was the young wife of Henry Bamford, one of the second generation of the family that founded the famous JCB firm. Emily often visited the Pinfold Street premises with her husband to talk to the factory 'hands'. It is not known why her ghost should continue to haunt the premises, although one story alleges that she actually died at the factory during one of her visits.

Visitors to the George and Dragon

WHEN Julie Crutchley was a girl of six, her family moved into the George and Dragon public house in Carter Street, Uttoxeter. The building had three floors, the upper one being an unused attic. In 1974 the attic was renovated, and Julie moved into the larger of the two attic bedrooms.

It was shortly after this that she began to see the three ghosts. There was a solemn-looking man who appeared to be in his mid-thirties, an elderly woman and a young boy. She didn't see them all together very frequently, but the woman often stood by Julie's bed smiling at her, and the boy would usually sit on the floor. The man always kept his distance and would just walk away.

'It seemed whenever I woke in the night and looked over my covers,' Julie recalls, 'I saw one of them. I was very scared as you can imagine, and quickly went back under the covers.'

She told her parents about her ghostly visitors, but they dismissed them as inventions of her childish imagination. However Julie continued to see these visitors until the family left the George and Dragon in 1980. Now an adult living in Kent, Julie looks back on her childhood and the three ghosts, and states, 'I have to say, with my hand on my heart, that what I saw was not in any way a figment of my imagination.'

The whole story was recently recalled for Julie when her sister Wendy contacted her. The George and Dragon has been converted into a number of bedsit flats, and one of the present tenants recently asked Wendy whether the place was haunted when it was a pub. Apparently, the ghosts are back!

104

WALSALL

The Hand of Glory

THE White Hart, a Jacobean inn at Caldmore Green, has long had a reputation for being haunted. In the 1950s, the pub landlord found a handprint in the dust on a table in a locked attic, when he knew that no one could enter the room without asking him for the key. A previous tenant was one of many people to hear footsteps crossing the same attic, as well as experiencing the sensation of a hand resting on his shoulder.

These phenomena were believed to be related to the suicide of a young girl in the inn during the 18th century, and also to the strange finds made at the White Hart in 1870. The Cromwellian sword was an interesting discovery, but the mummified arm of a young child proved more sensational.

The local story grew that the macabre relic was linked with witchcraft, and it became known as the Hand of Glory. The witchcraft connection is quite possible, but it was not a Hand of Glory. That title is very specific and refers to the severed hand of a hanged criminal, waxed and oiled, and used as a candelabra in black magic rituals to awaken the dead.

The child's arm found in the White Hart was certainly not the hand of a hanged felon. One suggestion is that it was a medical specimen prepared for students of anatomy, but adherents of this school of thought have no explanation of why it was found with a 17th century sword in the inn.

And the landlord who found the handprint in the dust in the locked attic did report that it was the print of a very small hand!

WEST BROMWICH

Winding the Clocks

GLADYS SMITH lived in a Victorian house in the Cronehills area of West Bromwich for the whole of her married life, moving to the area with her husband Victor in 1936. She moved out in 1987, a year after Vic's death, to live in sheltered housing. Although they were never wealthy, they did manage to buy two antique clocks and these were Vic's pride and joy. One was a long-case clock which stood in the hall, and the other a brass carriage clock which was kept on the sideboard in the front room. This room was kept for best, and only used at Christmas or if someone extra special visited. 'Like the vicar,' Gladys told me with a chuckle.

It was Vic's job to wind the two clocks every evening, and he would never allow Gladys to touch them. 'He used to tell me that winding the clocks was his job. He probably thought I'd overwind them or something,' Gladys said. The result of this 'ban' was that when Vic died in 1986, Gladys couldn't bring herself to touch the clocks and they both stopped. 'It wasn't like that music hall song where the grandfather clock stops when the old man dies,' she explained. 'I knew darn well why they'd stopped – I'd neglected them.'

She didn't really miss them as she always used the electric clock in the kitchen for telling the time. 'To be honest, I enjoyed the peace and quiet when they stopped,' she said. 'They both had ever such a loud tick. Mind you, I knew Vic wouldn't have approved.'

About seven weeks after Vic's death, Gladys was lying in bed, reading her library book, when she heard a familiar sound. Someone was winding the long-case clock in the hall. She tiptoed out on to the landing and put on the hall light. No one was there, but the loud ticking told her that the clock was going again. She went downstairs and found to her amazement that the clock was showing the right time! 'Now how do you explain that?' she asked me. 'It had been stopped for weeks.'

On an impulse she went into the front room and checked the brass carriage clock. This one was ticking too, although it was some hours slow. Gladys says that she pushed the hands round until it too was showing the right time. She decided there and then that she was going to keep both clocks fully wound in future. 'I can take a hint,' she says with a laugh. The carriage clock is with her in her new home, and is still ticking. She had to get rid of the long-case clock when she left the house in the Cronehills, but she sold it to one of Vic's friends. 'He's another clock fanatic,' Gladys said, 'so Vic would be happy that it's in a good home.'

WETWOOD

Red Stockings of Broughton Hall

BROUGHTON HALL is half a mile from the village of Wetwood, on the road from Eccleshall to Loggerheads. The ghost of a young Cavalier at Broughton Hall rejoices in the colourful name of Red Stockings, due to the manner in which he met his death. The present hall was built in 1637 and has been described as the finest black and white building in the county, although there was a manor on the spot long before the Norman Conquest.

During the Civil War of 1642-46, the Broughton family were strongly Royalist, and when the young heir to the estate saw a Cromwellian patrol marching up his drive, he threw open the window and taunted the Roundheads, shouting defiantly, 'I am for the king!'

At this, one of the Parliamentarian soldiers fired a

musket at him, and the ball hit the young Cavalier, wounding him fatally. He crawled from the Long Gallery to an adjoining room, where he died. His life blood soaked his stockings, turning them red, before seeping into the wooden floorboards. The blood was so deeply ingrained into the floor that the stain remained visible until the boards were taken up and replaced in 1926.

The ghost of Red Stockings has been seen in the Long Gallery many times since that fateful day. One such occasion was in 1880, when the Yonge family from neighbouring Charnes Manor were visiting. The children of the two families were playing hide and seek. An eleven year old visitor decided to hide in the Long Gallery. She heard footsteps, but when they didn't come near her, she peeped out from her hiding place behind the oak door. She saw a young man with red stockings gazing out through the windows. Assuming it was one of the Broughton boys, she tiptoed past him and rushed down the main staircase.

At the foot of the stairs she found the boy she thought she had seen in the Long Gallery. She was extremely surprised, and asked him how he'd got there so quickly and without being seen. He stated that he'd never been in the gallery, and a loud argument began between the two of them. Lady Broughton overheard them and intervened to distract them, although she later told Miss Yonge's parents that the girl had indeed seen the ghost of Red Stockings.

Another sighting occurred in the Edwardian era, when guests had been invited to a formal evening party at Broughton Hall. One lady apologised when she entered, saying that she had not realised that it was to be a fancy dress party until she'd seen a guest dressed as a Cavalier with red stockings, standing in an upstairs window.

A third experience was that of a cleaner from Fair Oak, who was scrubbing the stairs. When she saw a young man in red stockings approaching, she moved her bucket to allow him to pass. She was petrified when the figure passed clean through her, and after this terrifying experience she refused to clean the stairs again, unless she was accompanied.

Sir Delves Broughton sold the hall in 1914, and it is now owned by the Franciscan Order of St Joseph; the nuns of that order still say prayers for the soul of the young man whose ghost is known as Red Stockings.

The Fingerless Ghost of Charnes Hall

CHARNES HALL, the home of the Yonge family mentioned above, has its own ghost. One night in the second half of the 17th century the figure of a young woman appeared, dressed in a shroud and bleeding profusely from the stump of a severed finger. The macabre sight had a rational though brutal explanation. The young woman had been very sick, and it was thought she was mortally ill. When she appeared to have died, her grieving husband placed her in her coffin in the family vault.

A greedy and unfeeling coachman, who knew that the lady's corpse would still be wearing her valuable ring, bribed the sexton to leave the door to the vault open. That night he entered the vault and prised open the coffin. He tried unsuccessfully to wrench the ring from the lady's finger. Since this manoeuvre failed, he took out a sharp knife and hacked off the finger to get at the ring. He was shocked when living blood poured from the open wound. When the 'corpse' sat up, he fled from the vault, still carrying the blood-stained ring.

The lady, who had not died but had actually been in a paralysing coma, staggered back to Charnes Hall and managed to tap on a window. Her husband looked out, only to see his 'dead' wife standing there, begging him to let her in because she was so cold! His feeling of utter terror gradually turned to relief and then to joy as he realised that his wife was alive after all. She recovered from her terrifying ordeal, and lived for many more years.

Although the coachman was caught and hanged, the ring was never found. The lady, whose first ghostly appearance had a rational explanation, began to be seen again after her actual death. The shrouded figure is recognisable by her missing finger, and has been seen over the centuries, searching the grounds of Charnes Hall for her stolen ring.

WOLVERHAMPTON

The Ghost in the Lincoln Bomber

STAFF who work at the Aerospace Museum at RAF Cosford, near Wolverhampton, often find that they have an extra unpaid helper. This is the ghost of a man dressed in RAF blue, who appears when they are working on a Lincoln bomber. He is entirely benevolent, and will pass tools, undo screws, and when he is there the work always goes well. Staff believe that the ghost wishes to get the Lincoln back into flying order.

There are several theories about the ghost's identity. One belief is that he was a former Spitfire fighter-pilot whose plane was once kept at the museum. The problem with this idea is that the Spitfire has been sent elsewhere, but the ghost has remained to work on the bomber. Another hypothesis is that he was the pilot of a plane that crashed nearby in the 1940s, with no survivors.

Whoever he was, one thing seems clear. His ghost works on the Lincoln bomber, in the belief that he will one day use it to take to the sky again.

Purdy of The Grand

THE Grand Theatre in Wolverhampton was opened in 1884, and like many theatres has its ghosts. One of them is a diminutive gentleman, seen by Joan Wright, a cleaner, in 1953 and by many others before and since. He is always immaculately dressed in a long cloak and top hat, wearing a watch and chain on his chest. Although small in stature, he has immense dignity and presence. Theatre staff are sure that he is Mr Purdy, who was the general manager at the Grand Theatre in the 1920s. He is an imposing figure, but everyone feels that he is very kind and has only benign intentions. They even report that if he is requested politely to go away because they are busy getting the theatre ready for a performance, he simply vanishes. He obviously still accepts that the smooth running of the Grand is the main priority and that takes precedence over his own manifestations!

Other ghosts at the Grand are more mischievous; in the upper circle bar glasses are turned over, drawers are opened, and the cash registers ring up amounts of money when no one is near them. Although these events are sometimes attributed to Mr Purdy, surely tricks like these would be beneath his dignity. It is said that the ghosts of several actors and actresses who had appeared on stage at the Grand during their lifetime love to revisit the scene of their former glory. It may be that the practical jokes would be more in their line.

One other strange ghostly manifestation at the theatre is the mysterious waft of lavender perfume noticed in and around the orchestra pit. This scent began to appear soon after a lady visitor, said to be the wife of a mayor of Wolverhampton, had a fatal accident there when she fell from the stage into the orchestra pit.

BIBLIOGRAPHY

The Natural History of Staffordshire Robert Plot, 1686
Customs, Legends & Superstitions of Staffordshire C. Poole, 1875
Staffordshire Charles Masefield, 1910
The Story of Staffordshire Mark Hughes, 1918
Staffordshire: Customs, Superstitions & Folklore F. W. Hackwood, 1924
The Friendship of Cannock Chase M. Wright, 1935
The Tale of Ipstones Rev F. Brighton, 1937
History of Burton upon Trent C. H. Underhill, 1941
Staffordshire Phil Drabble, 1948
History of Tutbury &Rolleston C. H. Underhill, 1949
Folk Tales of the West Midlands Frederick Grice, 1952
Forgotten Folk Tales of The English Counties Ruth Tongue, 1970
Shane Leslie's Ghost Book, 1955
Folklore & Customs of Rural England Margaret Baker, 1974
The Midlands: Legends & Folklore John Merrill, 1974
Staffordshire Dialect Words D. Wilson, 1974
Folklore, Myths & Legends of Britain – Readers Digest, 1977
British Folk Tales & Legends Katharine M. Briggs, 1977
Tales From The Past Tom Byrne, 1977
The Folklore Calendar George Long, 1977
The Folklore of Staffordshire Jon Raven, 1978
Curiosities of the Peak District & Derbyshire F. Rogers, 1979
Murders, Myths & Monuments of N. Staffs W. Jamieson, 1979
Some Ghosts of Staffordshire Rosalind Prince, 1981
British Folklore, Myths & Legends Marc Alexander, 1982
Burton-on-Trent on Old Postcards Sowerby & Farman, 1983
More Old Postcards of Burton-upon-Trent S & F, 1984
The Haunted Pub Guide Guy Lyon Playfair, 1985
Modern Mysteries of Britain Janet & Colin Bord, 1987
Staffordshire & The Black Country Michael Raven, 1988
Britain's Haunted Heritage J. A. Brooks, 1990
Ghosts & Legends of the Peak District David Clarke, 1991
Curiosities of Staffordshire Ros Prince, 1992
Curiosities of Derbyshire & The Peak District Frank Rodgers, 1992
Tales of Old Staffordshire, Kathleen Lawrence-Smith, 1992

DIALECT OF STAFFORDSHIRE

Abear/abide	Endure, tolerate
Act daniel	To lie low, to keep one's head down
Afore	Before
Afterings	Last drops of milk from a cow
Agate	Busy; active. Also on fire
Aired	Lukewarm
Akerspurls	The shoots of a potato
Along	On account of
Aimer	Nearer
Am yo'm?	Are you?
Amperlash	Cheekiness
Anna/onna	Are not, aren't
Annunst	Near
Apieces	In pieces
Arint	Around
Ashgrid/essgrid	Fire grate
Aside	Next to, beside
Asker	A newt
Ashen lip	Hare lip
Ax/ex	Ask
Axings	Wedding banns
Backbiters/backfriends	Flaps of skin under the fingernails
Backen	Keep back, delay
Back end	Late autumn
Backhanded	Left handed
Bagging	Food taken to work
Barleys	Children's shout of truce
Bartered up	Splashed with mud
Barton	Farmyard
Bass	Slate found in coal
Bassylow	A heap of slate
Bastyle	Workhouse
Baum	To rub on ointment
Be sed	Behave yourself, be told
Beak	Food spilled on clothes
Beaked up	Dirty
Bease	Cattle
Beck	Peak of a cap
Bedfast	Bedridden
Beleddy	Bloody
Belike	Maybe, probably
Bellock	To cry loudly, to bellow
Bellywiggle	Earwig

Belter	Anything huge
Besom	Young woman with a pert nature
Bibble	Pebble
Billy whiffing	Cheating
Bishoped	Burnt (said of milk)
Blart	To weep
Blatch	To punch or smack
Bletherhead	Stupid, daft
Blowbroth	A big talker, a bighead
Bobbing	Playing truant
Bo	Ball
Bobowler	Inebriated
Bock	To stare
Bodge	To pierce
Boffemble	To confuse
Boggart	Ghost
Bone	To steal
Bonk	A hillside, an incline
Bonny clapper	Sour milk
Bont	Rope
Boster	A big one
Bostid	Broken
Bosunned/bawsen	Full to bursting
Bottomly	Completely
Bowdle/bottle	Money
Bowk	Bucket
Brahma	A good one
Brat	Apron
Brevit/purvit	To stalk prey, to hunt
Bricks	Pavement
Brock	Broken
Brodgel	A domestic row
Buffle	Smoke that blows back down the chimney
Bull	Factory hooter
Bullnogger	Small fish
Bullstone	Whetstone
Bullyed	A tadpole
Bungey	Cowman
Buzzed	Late for work
Cack	Dung
Cade	Pet lamb, a spoiled child
Caggy onded	Left handed
Cagmag	Poor quality meat. Also a gossip
Canna/conna	Cannot, can't
Cant	To tell tales, to 'split'
Casey	A leather football
Casical	Casual

Casilty	Risky, unreliable
Cast	Late
Cawsey	Pavement
Charnock/chonnock/	
Chowie	A turnip
Chat	Small piece of coal
Chawl	Cooked meat
Chelp	To be cheeky. Also to nag
Chobble	To chew (often implying noisily)
Chommers	Teeth
Chopsing	Chatting
Chunner/chunter	To complain, to grumble
Clack	Adam's apple
Clammed/clemmed	Hungry
Cob	Sweat
Cockstride	A short distance
Cod	To tease
Codge	A poor repair. Also to copy
Collow	To blacken
Colly-wesson	Contrary, awkward, askew
Conk	Apple core
Cosna?	Can't you?
Clomb	Climbed
Crackin off	Happening. 'What's crackin off over there?'
Craft	A small field
Crit	Small potato
Crog on	Exaggerate, cheat
Crommer/crammer	A lie
Croodle	To huddle together
Crossomical	Irritating, perverse
Crowdley	Having a rough surface
Crutter	To crouch
Cunnyfogle	Deceit, cunning
Cuthering	Whispering
Dade	To support a toddling child by holding it under the arms
Dant	Poor coal, slack
Daub	To cheat
Daytaler	Odd job man
Deck it!	Stop it!
Delf-hole	Mine shaft
Delf rags	Mining clothes
(in) Dickey's meadow	Late
Dinged	Bruised or damaged (fruit)
Dodging	Hem
Doolally	Crazy

Doubt	Consider, reckon, as in 'I doubt it'll rain soon' (meaning that it will!)
Dout	Extinguish
Dowl	Soft facial hair
Drop on	To meet by chance
Drumble	Hole
Ducker	A small flat stone
Dunna	Don't
Dust?	Do you?
Dwine	To be off one's food
Easings	Eaves
Edscrag	The boss
Eftest	Nearest, easiest
Entry	Jitty, alley
Esses	Ashes
Ever a one	Anyone
Ever likely!	No wonder!
Facey	Cheeky
Fang	Grab
Fardel	To waste time
Fassen	Fasten
Fear	To terrify
Feasen	Hurry
Feg	Grass
Feke	A punch
Fergie	Lousy, infested
Fetch	To steal
Fewgle	To whistle
Feyther	Father
Firk	To delve, to probe
Fisses	Fists
Fitty	Cat
Flirt	To throw, to flick
Fode/fold	A yard. Also an alley
Foggers/fogs/foggy	First turn in a game
Fossen	The first one
Fost	First
Franked	Late for work
Franzy/fratchety	Bad-tempered
Fridgy	Itchy
Fried frogs	Sliced potato fried in batter
Frim	Crisp, fresh (of vegetables)
Fuffle	To make a fuss
Fun	Found
Gain	Skilful or active
Gallows	A rascal, a rogue

116

Gammitting	Acting silly
Gammy	Child's cart with pram wheels
Ganzy	Cardigan, pullover, jersey
Gawby	Farm labourer. Also a simpleton
Gedling pegs	Sliced new potato sandwiches
Gennel/jornal	Narrow alley
Gill-houter	Owl
Gilliver	Wallflower
Gin	Give
Glassback	A lazy worker
Glede	Glowing embers
Good-it	Shrove Tuesday
Goster/gostrel	A boaster
Graunch	To gnash one's teeth, or to crunch
Groop	A ditch
Grued in	Ingrained
Gully	A gosling. Also an alleyway
Han	Have
Hard faced	Bold, impudent
Hareshorn lip	Hare lip
Hasky	Very dry
Hays/haydies	Haws
Healings	Bedclothes. Also book covers
Hike	To jerk up, to beckon
Hob	Top of the fireplace. Also goblin, elf
Hob hirst	Wood-elf
Hullock	A fat or lazy person
Hutched up	Crowded together
Ike	To beckon
Ikey	Naughty
Illing/illen	Covers of a book. Also bedcovers.
Insense	To tell, to inform
Jacksharp	A small fish
Jeath	Death
Jed	Dead
Jib	To give in
Jig	A steep slope
Jilliwow/jalliwow	A witch
Jinny	A nightdress
Jinny-spinner	Crane fly, daddy longlegs
Jitty	A narrow alley
Jonnock	Genuine, fair
Jornal	A narrow alley
Jubous	Suspicious
Just now	Later on
Kabe	To glance over one's shoulder

Kedge	To steal
Keech	A pastry
Keem	To examine closely
Keemers	Spectacles
Keffle	A clumsy person
Kecks	Trousers
Kench	To sprain
Kimkamming	Gossiping
Kind	Sleek
Kindle/kittle	To give birth
Kissing bunch	Mistletoe, holly
Knobstick	A blackleg
Lad-launcing	Staying out late with boys (said about girls)
Laggy/lags	Last turn in a game
Lamp/leather	To beat, thrash
Lant	urine
Launcing	Staying out late
Lesser/lezzer	Meadow, field
Leckin can	Watering can
Lickerin	Competing in a game
Lickers	Game to see which child can run fastest, throw furthest, etc.
Lief/liefer	Rather
Lig	To lie (down). Also to lie (tell lies)
Ligger	Liar
Lilycock	Finishing time, knocking off time
Lobby	Stew
Lollock/lozzock	To lie around idly, to be lazy
Lollocker	Tongue
Lommock	Lump
Lug	A knot in the hair
Lumpies	Oatmeal porridge
Lungeous	Rough in appearance or behaviour
Made away	Suffering from a cold
Mawl/maw	A mallet
Mardy	Spoiled, whingey
Mardybum	Child who cries easily and often
Mashing	Wooing, courting
Maunch	To chew. Also to ill-treat; a real mess
Mawkin	Scarecrow
Mayhappen	Perhaps, maybe
Mazey	Dizzy
Meadowbout	Marsh marigold
Meegrum	An ugly face, a grimace
Mending	Recuperating, convalescing
Mezzled	Pimply

118

Midden/misken/mixen	Muckheap
Mither	To worry
Mogging up	Showing off
Moggy	A mouse. Also a calf
Monty	Precocious
Moppet	Moth. Also dark 'It'll soon be moppet'.
Motto/motty	An uninvited comment
Moudiwarp	A mole
Mowed up	Dirty
Mucker	To worry, to be confused
Mulligrub	To hit in temper
Mumchance	Silent and mournful
Nadgell	To whimper
Narky/nazzy	Bad-tempered
Nasher	A child full of mischief
Neb	Peak of a cap
Nesh	Weak, soft, delicate, cowardly
Nivey/niveytous	Mean with money
Noggers	Football boots
Nointer	A bad person, someone who deserves a good hiding
Nor	Than 'You've got more nor me'
Noup	To hit
Oak-achins	Acorns
Oction/ocky	Place ('All over the oction')
Odge	Stomach
On	Of ('all on it')
Ond	Hand
Onion	Nose
Ooman	Woman
Oozy	Hairy, covered in fluff
Opening	A narrow alley, a jitty, gennel
Ost	To try, to offer
Otty-motty	In suspense
Pail	To thrash
Parcel	A number, 'a fair few'
Parish oak cake	Charity
Peffled	Speckled
Petty	Outside lavatory
Piece	A sandwich
Pitbonk	Area near to the pitshaft at a coalmine
Pleck	Area of waste ground
Plunder	Work something out, consider
Podge	To push into the front of a queue
Podger	A queue-jumper
Poke	Wages, money

Potbonk	A pottery
Powk	A stye (on the eye)
Proker	Poker
Puddingbag street	Cul-de-sac
Puddled	Stupid
Purvit	To search thoroughly
Pussnets	Nets for catching rabbits
Puther	A cloud of smoke
Puthery	Close or sultry (weather)
Queedle	A see-saw
Queedling	Rocking on a chair
Quice	Wood pigeon
Rabbleyedded	Full of nonsense
Rag-mannered	Bad-tempered
Rammel	A mongrel
Randy	Drinking, making merry
Rapatag	A worthless or scruffy person
Raps	Intestines
Rattlechops/rattlebasket	A talkative person
Rawsy	Coarse, rough
Razzered	Exhausted
Reasty	Rancid
Reeve	To turn up (shirt sleeves, etc.)
Rid	To tidy
Rift	To burp
Right	To scold, reprimand
Rimson	To clean out
Rindle	A small stream
Rinkers	Black and white marbles
Rittling/rickling	Runt of the litter
Robble	Tangle
Rodney	A barge labourer. Also an idle person; a rest
Rods	Idleness
Rommel	Rubbish
Ronk	Sly, crafty
Routing	Wooing, courting
Shank/sank	To walk
Saucy	Cheeky. Also faddy, fussy (eater)
Sawney	A simpleton
Sawnit	Late for work
Scour	A ford
Scrabble	Scramble
Scrat	Scratch. Also a mean person
Scrawmer	A money grabber
Scrawp	Graze or scratch

120

Screen	Wooden settee
Scritty	Weather-beaten
Scuft	Slap
Scuven	Shovel
Seefly-sawfly	Slow-witted
Seg	A callous
Segs/seggy	Second turn in a game
Senna-tucked	Being stiff after sitting
Set	To let or lease
Shape for	To get ready to
Sharpshins	A smart Alec
Sheed	To spill
Sheldapple	Chaffinch
Shippen	Cowshed
Shotties	Marbles
Shraffruck	A rubbish heap
Shut	Spoiled
Shutting	Harvest supper given for farm workers
Siden	Out of true, not quite square
Skeedy/skeggy/skitty	Left-handed
Skell	Distorted
Skelp	To cuff someone's head
Sken/scan	To squint
Skewift	Crooked
Skinny	Miserly, mean
Skitter	To sprinkle
Skitty-paw	Left-handed
Skrike	To cry, weep
Slat	Throw
Slavvy	General farm worker
Slither pudding	Slipshod worker
Slopstone	A sink
Slow-walking bread	Currant bread (traditionally eaten after a funeral)
Smacks	Sliced potato fried in batter
Snap	Food taken to work
Snead	Handle of a scythe
Sneap	To snub
Snicket	Narrow alley
Snided up	Cluttered
Snigglebog	Tuft of strong wiry grass
Soakies	Bread and milk/bread and tea
Sock	Liquid manure
Sog	Slap
Sonnet	Late for work
Sooner	An expert
Sough	A drain or a flue
Souse	Brawn, meat from head of pig

121

Spadger/spudgock/spug	Sparrow
Sparrow bills	Shoe nails
Sparrowed	Hard up, penniless
Spon new	Brand new
(to) Springe	To jump with pain
Springes	Sharp pains, corns
Squab	A wooden sofa
Starving/starved	Very cold, frozen
Stirk	A year old calf
Stitherum	Tall stories, lies
Stonnies/stonts	Marbles
Stranger	Flake of soot falling into the hearth (foretells the arrival of a stranger to the house)
Strap	On credit, tick
Strug	A stranger, a stray pigeon
Surry	A friendly form of address (possibly from Sirrah)
Swick/swilk	To spill over
Sward	Rind of bacon
Swobsy	Fat
Swobson	A fat woman
Syke	Man who drinks at someone else's expense
Tack	A nasty taste
Tacky-bonk	A small hill; a pit mound
Tank/tonk	A blow
Tansel	To beat, to hit
Tantadlin	A fiddling job
Telled	Told
Think much on	To admire, to esteem
Think on	Remember
Thodden	Unrisen (of bread)
Thrades/threeds	Lots
Thrape	To hit, to beat
Throstle/throlly	Thrush
Thrutched	Crowded
Thrutching	Choking
Thurling	Beating
Timber-toed	Pigeon-toed
Tin and bonnet shop	Ironmongers
Tinkler	A restive person
Tissick	A ticklish cough
Tit	A horse
Tommy	Food
Tother	Frogspawn
Tow-rag	Oatcake
Trashers	Working boots

122

Tucks	Lots
Tuggies	Lice
Tump	A heap, a mound
Tun-dish	A funnel
Tussy	Stupid
Tweedle/tweezle	A see-saw
(a) Two-three	A few
Unscrewgle	To open (one's eyes)
Upbonk	Uphill
Urchin	A hedgehog
Us	We ('Us are going Burton')
Waft	Energy, stamina
Wanky	Weak
Waterlags	Pools standing in fields
Welly	Nearly
Werrent	Floor
Werrit	To worry
Wesh	Wash
Wetched	Web-footed
Wigging/wiggy	Any topping for bread (jam, bacon)
Without	Unless
Wo	Wall
Wom/wum	Home
Wom it	Go home
Wonder	An after-dinner snooze
Woppit	Wasp
Wozzin	Throat
Yammer	To complain
Yarbs	Herbs
Yawp	To speak loudly and raucously
Yed	Head
Yerrin	Herring
Yern	Heron
Yo	You
Yo'm	You are
Youther	A youth

INDEX